swim home

Searching for the Wild Girl of Champagne

KATHLEEN MCDONNELL

◆ FriesenPress

Suite 300 - 990 Fort St
Victoria, BC, V8V 3K2
Canada

www.friesenpress.com

Copyright © 2020 by Kathleen McDonnell
First Edition — 2020

All rights reserved.

No part of this publication may be reproduced in any form, or by any means, electronic or mechanical, including photocopying, recording, or any information browsing, storage, or retrieval system, without permission in writing from FriesenPress.

ISBN
978-1-5255-6847-3 (Hardcover)
978-1-5255-6848-0 (Paperback)
978-1-5255-6849-7 (eBook)

1. HISTORY, MODERN, 18TH CENTURY

Distributed to the trade by The Ingram Book Company

"When I was perhaps eight years old I began to like to swim. If we were living near where a river flowed by, we girls would always swim."

-from *The Autobiography of a Fox Indian Woman*, 1918

TABLE OF CONTENTS

CHAPTER 1 1
Crossing the Wapsipinicon

CHAPTER 2 7
Monkey Girls and Gazelle Boys

CHAPTER 3 17
A Dip in Memmie's Moat

CHAPTER 4 25
The Learned Men and the Secretary

CHAPTER 5 37
The Surgeon and the Scholar

CHAPTER 6 49
The Librarian, the Mayor, and the Vigneron

CHAPTER 7 65
A Life Like No Other

CHAPTER 8 81
The Lone Woman

CHAPTER 9 91
Women Between Worlds

CHAPTER 10 105
The Red Earth People

Chapter 11 117
The Last Tribe of Iowa

CHAPTER 12 131
Lost Daughter of the Red Earth People

CHAPTER 13 137
Marie-Angelique was Here

NOTES ON SOURCES. 149
APPENDIX (The Wolf Sisters) 158
ACKNOWLEDGEMENTS. 165

CHAPTER 1
Crossing the Wapsipinicon

January 2018

Independence is a mid-size town in the northeast quadrant of the state of Iowa. The Mississippi, which forms the border between Iowa and Illinois, flows about fifty miles to the east. A river of much more modest proportions, the Wapsipinicon, runs right through town. In fact, because the Wapsie (as it's affectionately known by the locals) takes a sharp, almost ninety-degree bend, as you drive through Independence you cross it twice, once on the outskirts and again in the center of town.

Wapsipinicon. The name is pronounced exactly as it's spelled. I can still hear my dad saying the word. As a kid, I thought it sounded very funny. But I know now that it's an Indigenous place-name, and simply unfamiliar to my ears. The local histories like to tell a legend of dubious provenance, a Romeo-and-Juliet story of star-crossed lovers from different tribes:

> "*Wapsi, a young warrior, and Pinicon, the daughter of an Indian chief, eloped, but were found by Pinicon's father and the other chiefs. The couple decided they would rather die*

> *than be taken back and separated. They raced to the river, clasped each other, leaped into the stream, and drowned in the swirling waters. The sorrowful Indian chief later named the stream Wapsipinicon."*

The "legend" is, of course, a sentimental fabrication, cooked up by white people who settled here nearly 200 years ago. In fact, the name comes from *wapasi' piniaki*, the name in the Meskwaki language for the swan potato, an arrowhead plant that once grew in abundance along the riverbank. Meskwaki women and children periodically came here to harvest the swan potato for its large, edible root. At least they did until the mid-nineteenth century, when the Meskwaki Nation was forced to leave their ancestral lands and move west.

Mind you, Iowa isn't exactly a prime destination for Canadians, certainly not in January, in the middle of the fiercest cold snap in recent memory. Partly I was here for research, on a quest to learn more about a woman born more than three centuries ago, who may have been one of those children gathering swan potatoes. But the main reason my spouse Alec and I were here was to attend the funeral of my Aunt Virginia, the last of my late father's twelve siblings.

We drove along First Street, past the Iowa State Bank, past the public library, past the Pizza Hut and the Subway and the McDonald's. We turned onto Golf Course Blvd., where a bakery called Kathy's Kakes provided special-occasion pastries for the locals. We were driving a bit north and west of town, in search of the farmhouse where my father grew up. I had visited there a few times as a child, but the farm had passed out of family hands many years ago. We had only a vague idea where we were headed, but my cousin Jay had said to keep an eye out for a large, white house with six front windows and a wraparound porch. We stopped at one that fit the description, where a fellow in the driveway was transferring grain from a big tank into a truck. We asked if he knew anything about the history of the house and its former inhabitants.

"What's the name?" he asked, and when I replied, "McDonnell," he broke into a wide grin.

"Yep, that's it. Gertie McDonnell. I used to clear the drainpipes for her."

So, he remembered my Aunt Gert, who had lived in the house until the late seventies. It turned out he owned the land on one side of the driveway, which used to be part of the farm. He urged me to go knock on the door and introduce myself to the current occupant, whose name was Leslie. Leslie, though, was less welcoming than Grain Guy had been. I think she was afraid I was going to ask to come in and look around the house, which I would have liked to do. But I reassured her that we just wanted to walk around the grounds and take a few photos. She looked visibly relieved as we drove off a few minutes later.

Back in Independence, as we walked around town, I noticed a somewhat forlorn-looking sign saying, "Buchanan County Genealogical Society," which pointed to the rear door of a municipal building. We entered and found ourselves in a cavernous garage with several parked fire trucks and a sign indicating that the Genealogical Society was in the basement. We went downstairs, fully expecting to find it closed, but we lucked out; Thursday was one of two afternoons in the week the Society was open. Inside was a large, single room lined with cabinets containing drawers full of three-by-five-inch file cards, the kind libraries used in the days before everything was digitized. Truly, the place looked like the Land that Time (and the Internet) Forgot.

The proprietor, whose name was Bob, clearly wasn't expecting any visitors, much less a couple from Canada. But he was pleased to be of service and set right to work, opening drawer after drawer and pulling out file cards. In a matter of minutes, he managed to locate the obituaries of my father and all but two of his siblings, plus a copy of their parents' – my grandparents – certificate of marriage. From a separate cabinet with wide, flat drawers for oversize documents, he pulled out a map of Buchanan County in the late 1800s, indicating the owners of the various farm plots.

I took out my phone to start taking photos of the documents, but Bob shook his head. "We prefer photocopies. I'll do them for you."

I took it as further evidence of the time-warp this place seemed to inhabit. But he hastened to add that charging for photocopying was one of the only ways the volunteer-run group could bring in revenue. He added that he was very proud of the Society's vintage photocopier, which he judged superior to the newer digital models.

"Been running for years without any problem."

We watched the sheets tumble into the receiving tray with smooth efficiency. Yes, we had to admit that this machine looked like it could soldier on for years to come.

Bob slid the stack of photocopies into an oversized envelope and handed it to me. The total charge came to the princely sum of seven dollars. We gave him a twenty-dollar bill and told him the rest was a donation to the Society.

In the car I laid out the map and took a closer look. There, in the lower-left quadrant, were two adjacent plots, one marked "J. Burns," the other "J. McDonnell." The Wapsipinicon River snaked right across both of them, just as my dad had said. At the time, I didn't fully appreciate the significance of what I was looking at. Only gradually did I come to understand what the map was showing me; that I had a more direct connection to Marie-Angelique Memmie LeBlanc, the Wild Girl of Champagne, than I ever imagined.[1]

For more than ten years I had been obsessed with this woman and her extraordinary life. This book is an account of an odyssey full of twists and turns, one that's taken me from the cornfields of Iowa to a centuries-old *chateau* on the other side of the Atlantic Ocean. Marie-Angelique, the girl who spent ten years surviving in

---

1 In France the Wild Girl is invariably referred to as Marie-Angelique. Writers in English, myself included, have mistakenly assumed that Memmie was a diminutive or nickname, when in fact it was the name of the first bishop of Chalons in the third century CE. Throughout this book I will use both names, depending on context, etc. though I now generally defer to the French usage and favor Marie-Angelique. Of course, both are versions of her European name. Her birth name is lost to history.

the wild, who socialized with royalty and became a fine lady, who was an object of fascination for the major intellectuals of her day. What writer wouldn't get caught in the grip of such a story? I'd spent a good part of the past decade writing a play about her, into which I poured many of my own fears and preoccupations – especially my love of swimming. Until I got stuck, not from writer's block, but from a growing sense that this woman's life wasn't mine to create.

In the beginning, though, it was all about stories about feral children, and my fascination with them.

CHAPTER 2
Monkey Girls and Gazelle Boys

"On trouvé sur le haut d'un arbre fort élevé, dans un cimitière, près de Vitry, une fille sauvage d'environ dix ans. Elle ne se nourrit que de feuilles d'ormes, de grenouilles et de chair crüe que devore avec avidité. Elle courre comme un lièvre, et grimpe comme un chat."

-From December, 1731 issue of the gazette *Mercure de France*

The above quote is the earliest recorded mention of the person who would become known as the Wild Girl of Champagne. It's taken from a report from a city in the Champagne district, about the discovery of a female child in a cemetery outside near the village of Vitry. It notes that the girl, who appeared to be about ten years of age, was found sitting on a branch of a tree, and offers a few other startling observations about her: "She eats nothing but the leaves of wild plants, frogs and raw flesh which she consumes with great relish. She runs like a hare and climbs trees like a cat." Clearly, this was no ordinary foundling.

As it turned out, there had been an earlier sighting of a similar creature by residents of the nearby village of Songy in September 1731. The villagers were frightened by the appearance of the creature, who was clothed in animal skins, covered with matted, unkempt hair, and wielding a small club with mysterious markings on it. Certain that it was some kind of demon, one of the villagers ordered his bulldog to attack. As the dog leapt toward it, the creature lifted the bludgeon and brought it down full force on the snarling dog's head, instantly killing it. When they finally managed to overpower the demon, the villagers realized, to their utter astonishment, that the creature was human – a female child, to be precise.

Various accounts of her first days in the village are similarly shocking: Taken to the local nobleman's estate, the girl ran into the kitchen, pulled down a chicken carcass hanging from the ceiling, and proceeded to devour it raw. Her eyes were in constant motion, darting from one side to another, and she made "no sound but the calls of birds."

She became known as the Wild Girl of Champagne, the eighteenth-century equivalent of a media sensation. Her fame spread like wildfire. People came from all over to see this bizarre specimen for themselves, creating a circus atmosphere reminiscent of what would happen with Canada's Dionne quintuplets in the 1930s. Wild rumours circulated that she had superhuman strength and was the spawn of a tribe of cannibals. As for where she had come from, early observers concluded that she was likely a "member of one of the savage races" residing in Africa. When, after an attempt to escape, she was discovered sleeping outside in the bitter cold with no ill effects, speculation shifted to the far northern latitudes of the Americas.

She was administered the sacrament of baptism in June 1732 and was given the names Memmie, for the patron saint of Chalons, and LeBlanc, a common surname in that part of France. There's some uncertainty about how she acquired her given name. Some accounts allege that she remembered being called Marie-Angelique in her former life. She was subjected to a bloodletting treatment, to "get some good French blood in her veins" and cure her of her wild behaviors. But whatever taming effect the bloodletting had must have worn off quickly. Despite the servants' efforts to restrain her, she would sometimes strip naked and dive into the moat surrounding the estate.

Among the Wild Girl's many celebrity visitors was the queen of Poland, who decided to take her on a hunting expedition, saying, "She is a child of nature, it will make her happy to run free again." No sooner had the royal hunting party set out than the Wild Girl ran off, returning a short time later with the warm body of a hare, dripping with blood, which she deposited at the queen's feet. The incident could well be the earliest use of the phrase, "The queen was not amused."

Humans have had an enduring fascination with the feral-child narrative. These stories have emerged again and again through history, perhaps most famously with Romulus and Remus, the mythical twins who, abandoned as infants, were suckled by a she-wolf and went on to establish the city of Rome. In modern times several of these stories have become well known, especially through cinema. François Truffaut's famous 1970 film *L'Enfant Sauvage* dramatizes a French doctor's efforts to civilize and educate Victor, a boy found in the woods near Aveyron in 1798. A mute teenager who appeared in the city of Nuremburg a couple of decades later, became the subject of German director Werner Herzog's 1974 film *The Enigma of Kaspar Hauser*. But there are scores of other lesser-known cases, many of them occurring in our own time: A ten-year-old boy was found living with a herd of gazelles in the Syrian desert in the early 1950s. Four decades later, a girl was discovered in Ukraine living with a pack of dogs. These stories tend to follow a certain pattern: The earliest reports announce in a breathless, tabloid-style tone the discovery of a child "living with" or "raised by" wild animals. Over time, the initial reports give way to a more realistic narrative, often involving disability, parental abandonment and sometimes outright falsehood.

That was certainly the case with a story that hit the media while I was working on this book, about a girl reportedly living with monkeys in the forests of northern India. Under headlines trumpeting a "modern-day *Jungle Book*" news reports said the girl, aged around eight, had no toilet habits, no speech, crawled on all fours and screeched at passersby. Some accounts described a pitched battle in which police had to fight off a whole herd of monkeys in order to rescue her. But over the next few days the story began to unravel with the hyper-speed of the Internet age, and the monkey-girl story was soon debunked. Officials in the state of Uttar Pradesh said the girl was actually found on a roadside near the forest, not deep in the wilderness. Though there were monkeys in the vicinity, they confirmed that forest rangers did not, in fact, find the girl living with monkeys. Her improvement over the next few days – especially her rapid transition from crawling to walking normally – led doctors to conclude that she hadn't been in the forest since birth and had been raised by humans after all.

The truth of the matter was infinitely sadder and had nothing to do with wild animals. It turned out that the child had been abandoned by her family, who didn't want to look after her because she was female and developmentally delayed. "Some families value girls less than boys," said Ranjana Kumari a leading activist against female feticide. "They would rather get rid of the girl than spend money on her." As if to drive the point home, one Indian newspaper's account contained some "scientific" childbearing tips, including advice to "eat mutton to conceive boys."

At first glance, the story of Marie-Angelique LeBlanc fits squarely into the feral-child narrative tradition. The early accounts of her appearance in Songy speak of her animal-like behaviours; climbing trees, making bird calls, skinning frogs alive, and eating them raw. But this particular Wild Child upends the pattern, not least because, in her case, those early reports turned out to be quite accurate. In many ways the Wild Girl of Champagne never fit all that comfortably into the feral-child paradigm, and those who study the phenomenon haven't quite known what to do with her. For generations her story has lain tucked away, accompanied by an invisible asterisk, alongside the gazelle boys and wolf children.

The Wolf Children
My own fascination with these stories was heartily fed by a book by British writer Michael Newton called *Savage Girls and Wild Boys: A History of Feral Children*. I was familiar with some of the cases Newton wrote about, but I was particularly taken with two that were completely new to me. One was that of Marie-Angelique Memmie Le Blanc, the Wild Girl of Champagne. The other was Newton's account of Amala and Kamala, two real-life wolf children.

In 1920, the Reverend J.A. L. Singh, a Christian cleric in India, reported that he had rescued two girls, aged about eight years and eighteen months, from a wolves' den. Singh took the girls to his orphanage in the district of Midnapore. In his diary Singh recorded their distinctly wolf-like behaviours. They would not allow themselves to be dressed, rejected cooked food, and scratched and bit people who tried to feed them. Both girls had developed thick calluses on their palms and knees from and walking on all fours. They were mostly nocturnal, had an aversion to sunshine, and could see very well in the dark. They also exhibited an acute sense of smell and an enhanced ability to hear. The girls craved the taste of raw meat, ate out of a bowl on the ground, and appeared to be insensitive to cold and heat. At night they would howl, calling out, Singh deduced, to their wolf family. They did not speak and appeared to be regulating their body temperatures by sticking out their tongues, like cats.

Singh took up the daunting task of rehabilitating them into human society. He recorded his observations in his diary over a period of nearly ten years, replete with photos. His efforts yielded scanty results. After a few months at the orphanage, Amala, the younger child, died of a kidney infection. Despite his initial impression that the girls exhibited no human emotions, Singh noted that Kamala showed signs of mourning at Amala's death. Eventually she was partially house-trained, learned to speak a few words, and became used to the company of other human beings. After years of hard work, she was able to walk upright, though never proficiently, and she often reverted to all fours when she needed to go somewhere quickly. Kamala only lived to the age of seventeen, dying of tuberculosis in 1929.

If accurate, Singh's account would represent one of the best documented efforts to observe and rehabilitate feral children. But controversy dogged the story from the time it first became public. The *New York Times* reported in October 1926 that an argument over the veracity of Singh's account "brought the members of a well-known London club to fisticuffs." Notable scientists like British biologist Julian Huxley and American anthropologist Robert M. Zingg publicly declared support for Singh's story. Zingg even co-authored a 1942 book with Singh, *Wolf-children and Feral Man*. But another prominent anthropologist, Ashley Montagu, wrote a stinging review of their book, calling Singh a "naïve but honest person" whose observations largely "belong to the realm of folklore." Montagu argued that his reports of the wolf-children should not be accepted as science, "based on the unsupported testimony of one person, Mr. Singh." In the 1950s Bruno Bettelheim, perhaps the most respected psychological expert in the U.S., weighed in on the controversy, arguing that Kamala and Amala, and indeed most so-called feral children, were actually cases of severe autism. In later decades, Bettelheim's reputation plummeted when his claim that autism was caused by so-called "refrigerator mothers" was completed discredited. But one thing he was right about was the prevalence of autism and other developmental delays in feral-children cases.

One of the many similarities between the wolf children and the most recent monkey-girl report is their locale, the Indian subcontinent. These accounts were particularly abundant among nineteenth-century British imperialists, who were drawn to stories that confirmed their beliefs about their Indian subjects – that they were childish and animal-like. There is a powerful appeal in the view, inherited from Rousseau and the eighteenth-century Romantics, that there is a fundamental, "pure" state of human nature that has been distorted by civilization. Like *The X-Files'* Agent Mulder, we *want* to believe in the myth of the noble savage. Ashley Montagu admits as much in his review of Singh and Zingg's book: "I should very much like to believe the greater part of this story."

I was similarly taken with this romantic view of feral children. By the time I encountered the wolf-children story, I'd had a twenty-year career writing about and for young people, much of it in the folk- and fairy-tale vein. Drawing on Singh's account of his work with Amala and Kamala, I wrote a contemporary fairy tale called *The Wolf Sisters*, exploring the theme of wildness vs. civilization. I chose different names for the protagonists and added other fictional elements. At the end of my story, one of the sisters returns to live with the wolves, while the other accepts her human-ness and chooses to remain with the Singh character, whom I called the Teacher. (The complete text of the story appears in the Appendix at the back of this book.)

I took the story to a theater company I'd worked with on some of my earlier plays, which resulted in a commission to write a new piece on the broad theme of feral children. I decided the wolf girls would be the main focus, but the script would also incorporate other feral children from history as minor characters. After several drafts and a workshop, it became clear that the piece wasn't jelling, at least not in its current form. By mutual agreement the project was set aside, a not-infrequent fate of plays-in-development. Still, I found it hard to give up on the piece, mostly because one of those "minor" characters had gotten her hooks into me. As it turned out, it was just as well that the play itself never came to fruition. I learned that stories about wolf-children almost invariably raise red flags.

Debunker-in-chief

In 2008, a sensational hoax involving wolves and a child became public. *Survival with Wolves: A Memoir of the Holocaust Years* had been published to acclaim in the late nineties. The book's author, Misha Defonseca, said the book was an account of her experiences as an eleven-year-old Jewish child during World War II. It chronicled her escape from Nazi-occupied Belgium in 1941, after which she spent the next four years walking, by herself, through the forests of Europe. On her journey she was befriended by a pack of wolves, to whose care and protection she owes her survival.

Even before publication, there were warnings about serious credibility issues with Defonseca's story. But publication went ahead, with enthusiastic blurbs from Nazi-hunter Elie Wiesel and an endorsement from the North American Wolf Foundation. *Survival with Wolves* became a best-seller, was translated into eighteen languages, and was adapted for an Italian opera and a French feature film. Oprah was interested. Disney bought an option on the English-language film rights. But amid mounting evidence and a growing a chorus of skeptics, it all came unravelled. Defonseca confessed that her real name was Monique de Wael, that she hadn't lived with a pack of wolves to escape the Nazis, and that she hadn't trekked 1,900 miles across Europe in search of her deported parents. To top it all off, she was Catholic, not Jewish. *Survival with Wolves* wasn't just exaggeration; it was made up out of whole cloth.

Despite Defonseca's defense that the book contained metaphorical truth – "not actual reality, but my reality, my way of surviving" – *Survival with Wolves* joined the ranks of bogus Holocaust memoirs. The most famous of these "memoirists" is Jerzy Kozinski, whose 1965 book *The Painted Bird* was considered a major work of Holocaust literature until it was exposed as largely fictionalized in the early 1980s. The irony is that many Holocaust accounts of survival in the wild are factually true, telling of panicked parents who really did send their children to hide in the woods as the Nazis invaded their villages. One vivid account is a memoir by Alex Levin, *Under the Yellow and Red Stars*. In 1942, ten-year-old Levin and his older brother hid in the woods of Poland for more than eighteen months. Levin attributes their survival not to mythical wild animals, but to luck and to the forest itself, which he calls his "best friend... my saviour and faithful benefactor."

One of the most authoritative debunkers of *Survival with Wolves* was a French surgeon named Serge Aroles. He called out Defonseca for recycling what he called "the usual surrealist clichés" about children who live with wolves. With his medical background, Aroles was able to challenge her account of her time with the animals. (Defonseca had told of wounds healed by wolf saliva, which she claimed was a natural antiseptic.) As I learned when I came across his book *L'enigme des Enfants-loups: Une Certitude Biologique Mais un Déni des Archives* ("The enigma of wolf-children: a biological certainty but a denial of the archives") Serge Aroles had made something of a career of being debunker-in-chief. In the book, a survey of feral-children stories since medieval times, he concludes that almost all of the accounts of wild children – even some of the most famous ones like Victor of Aveyron – were, to varying degrees, false. He painstakingly examined dozens of these accounts, exposing their weaknesses – mistaken beliefs, poor documentation – as well as the outright frauds and deliberate hoaxes, often for monetary gain. "The forest," Aroles stated, "is the largest orphanage in the history of mankind." As with Defonseca's story, Aroles' medical background gave his arguments the stamp of authority. For example, he gives a detailed analysis of the nutritional content of the milk of various animals – wolf, bear, primates – and concludes that there is no way a human infant could survive on them.

To my chagrin I discovered that the story of Amala and Kamala fell squarely into Aroles' hoax category. In *L'enigme des Enfants-loups* he offers extensive evidence of deliberate fraud on the part of Rev. Singh: The original diary which he claimed to have written "day after day during the life of the two wolf-girls" was, in fact, written after 1935, six years after Kamala's death. The photos showing the two girls walking on all fours and eating raw meat were taken in 1937, after both girls had died. In fact, according to the medical doctor in charge of the orphanage, all of the girls' wolf-like characteristics – sharp, long teeth, walking on all-fours, nocturnal vision with emission of an intense blue glare – were pure inventions by Singh, who was desperate to raise money to keep his struggling orphanage afloat.

After plowing through *L'enigme des Enfants-loups*, which was never translated into English, I realized that I'd dodged a bullet. If I'd finished the play about the wolf girls and it had been publicly performed, I probably would have had to face some embarrassing questions. As Defonseca had learned the hard way, association with the word "hoax" is not a good look for an author. In *L'enigme des Enfants-loups*, Aroles pokes holes in nearly every story, exposing a wealth of errors, poor documentation, and outright fabrication. But as fate would have it, he singles out one story as authentic; the one case in history of a truly feral child being rehabilitated. It was the very character who wouldn't let go of me; Marie-Angélique Memmie Le Blanc, the Wild Girl of Champagne.

CHAPTER 3

A Dip in Memmie's Moat

In the fall of 2009, I went with my spouse Alec on a dream trip – three weeks in the south of France. Our younger daughter, Ivy, joined us in Paris, where we planned to spend a few days before flying back to Canada. At that point I'd done a fair amount of research into the Wild Girl's story and had just gotten started on the play I wanted to write about her. I don't know why I hadn't thought of it earlier, but once in Paris I realized we were only a couple of hours away from the Champagne district, the place where Marie-Angelique first emerged in 1731. On our last full day in France, we booked train tickets to Reims, where we rented a car and drove a half-hour south of the city.

We'd seen many lovely places during our time in France, but the village of Songy was, not to put it too unkindly, unremarkable. There was a lovely old church, of course. But where was the bustling square surrounded by cafés and *brasseries*? Where was the *boulangerie* with pastries and fresh-baked baguettes in the window? Songy looked to be not much more than a single street, bordered by a stone wall on one side. There were houses, a few cars parked here and there. But not a living soul to be seen. I began to feel foolish, coming here with so little forethought, so little time.

We parked the car and walked through a little courtyard leading to the church. The heavy front door was unlocked, so we went in. We'd been in a lot of old churches in France – there's at least one in every village – and though this twelfth-century structure was a gem; it didn't make much of an impression on me. Maybe I had old-church fatigue. Alec and Ivy were still looking around the interior when I decided to go back outside. I exited through the side door, and that's when I saw the statue.

It was in the middle of a small, grassy plot beside the church; a statue of a young woman in bare feet with long, flowing hair. There was a kind of sling hanging from her shoulder, in which she carried what looked like sticks of wood. It was a fairly generic depiction of a pastoral figure, one that could have been – and likely was – purchased from a garden shop. There was no plaque, nothing to indicate who the figure was supposed to represent, or why she was here. But I had a pretty good idea.

Just then a man came out of one of the nearby buildings – finally, a human presence! As he walked toward one of the parked cars, I called out to him in awkward French, asking if he could tell me anything about the statue. He answered in a rapid flow of words that whizzed right by me, except for one phrase: *la fille sauvage*.

"C'est elle?" I called out. "C'est la fille sauvage?"

"Oui!" he shouted and launched into more rapid French as he pointed to a stone wall on the other side of the road. I looked where he was pointing and noticed a stone tower at one end of the wall. I recognized immediately it from the photos on the Internet. It was the *chateau* where Marie-Angelique LeBlanc, *la fille sauvage* herself, had lived for a time after she emerged from the woods in September of 1731.

I could see that the man was beginning to get impatient with my poor French. He was trying to tell me to go to the building across the road. I pointed, shouting, "La?" to let him know I understood.

"Oui, oui, la!" He nodded vigorously as he got into the car.

Alec, Ivy, and I crossed the road and passed through the gate. Another empty courtyard. Why had the man told us to come here?

There was a door off to our right, and Alec went to knock on it. I was nervous, reluctant, but we'd come this far, what choice did we have? At least I knew that Alec's French was up to the task of an apology to whoever was living there.

A woman opened the door. She was short, with a finely etched face. She thought we were there to buy wine – it turned out the *chateau* was now a winery, a *cave à Champagne* – but when Alec got to the words *la fille sauvage*, her manner changed. She grew animated and began to speak very fast, explaining that her husband would very much like to speak with us. He was away at the moment but would be back very soon. Could we please come back in, say, half an hour?

I looked at Alec. We didn't have a lot of time. We had to drive back to Reims, drop off the rental car, and catch the 5:30 train back to Paris.

"Of course we will come back," he replied to the woman.

We repaired to a café in the village up the road, where a cold buffet disabused us of the notion that it's impossible to find a bad meal in France. Nearly an hour had elapsed by the time we got back to the *cave à Champagne*. We saw the woman and her husband waiting in the courtyard. They waved and came forward to greet us as we parked the car. He introduced himself as Eric Phelizon and his wife as Marie-Ange. They ushered us inside, into a large room with a long table, on which sat several bottles of their own small-batch variety champagne. Marie-Ange opened one, poured it into tall-stemmed glasses, and set one before each of us. We drank and she refilled, several times over, from a second and then a third bottle, which contained a pale rose-coloured liquid. They offered us chocolates, nuts, *madeleines*.

For most of my adult life, I'd thought of champagne as a boring beverage that gets brought out for toasts on special occasions. As for pink bubbly, well, that was only fit for girls' night out. But now I could see how wrong I had been. This tongue-dancing drink was a revelation. Instantly I acquired a new appreciation for sparkling wines – the good stuff, that is – and since that day my attitude has shifted 180 degrees. Bring on the bubbly, the pinker and girlier the better.

But this was not an afternoon to fritter away on small talk and wine. There was another subject of burning interest that had brought us to this place, a subject that – it quickly became clear – preoccupied Eric Phelizon almost as much as making wine; the fabled Wild Girl of Champagne, Marie-Angelique Memmie LeBlanc.

I explained in my halting French that that I was writing a play about *la fille sauvage*, that we'd come to Songy specifically because of its connection to her story.

Eric left the room and quickly returned with a file folder, thick with dog-eared sheets of paper. He launched into a full summary on the facts of Marie-Angelique's remarkable story – how she was discovered living in the woods near Songy in 1731, wearing nothing but animal skins. How she ran like a hare, climbed trees like a cat. How her eyes seemed to look everywhere at once. How she killed a bulldog with a single blow of her club, terrifying the villagers, who ran about screaming, "The devil has come to Songy!"

Eric and Marie-Ange (whose name's similarity to that of *la fille sauvage* did not escape me) spoke almost no English, which would normally have been a stumbling block. But I was so familiar with the story that I was easily able to follow their French. As I nodded eagerly, it became clear to Eric that I already knew everything he was telling me about Memmie LeBlanc. Did I know that she refused to eat anything but roots and raw meat? "Yes," I assured him. "I knew that." That she had extraordinary tolerance for the cold? "Yes, that, too." Did I know of her habit of tearing off her clothing and jumping into the moat whenever she felt like it? That the local viscount's servants had to constantly restrain her from doing so? Of course, I knew all that!

I could see that Eric was beginning to understand that he'd found a *compatriote*, someone who knew as much about – who *cared* as much about – this mysterious woman and her centuries-old, largely-forgotten story.

Swim Home

Turned out we weren't alone in our keen interest. "Franck Rolin!" Eric exclaimed. "Franck Rolin is the man you must talk to! He knows everything about *la fille sauvage*."

I noted the name in my notes but had no idea who this person was and what he might add to my already extensive research.

We asked about the statue. Eric and Marie-Ange explained that it had been purchased by the mayor, who hoped to use Memmie's story to put Songy on the map – the tourism map, to be specific. But he hadn't gotten around to getting a plaque made for it yet, and the hordes of visitors eager to learn about *La Fille Sauvage* were yet to materialize. (It dawned on us that *we* were the hordes.)

An hour or more passed. We went on talking, drinking champagne, nibbling madeleines. We decided to skip our train and catch the next one. We skipped that one, too, and finally had to inform Eric and Marie-Ange that if we didn't get on the road very soon, we'd miss the last train back to Paris. We headed toward our rental car, but Eric said he had something to show us first. He led us through a field scattered with dried-out corncobs, left behind, he said, by wild boars who feasted on them. At one end of the field was a deep trench filled with water, stretching about half the length of a football field. Eric explained that this was part of his ongoing effort to restore the estate to the way it was in Marie-Angelique's time.

Yes, Eric Phelizon was digging a moat – Memmie's moat; the one the servants had tried so hard to keep her out of.

By now we were really in danger of missing our train. But a thought came over me – this was an opportunity I couldn't pass up. I swim whenever, wherever I can – mostly in oceans, lakes; fairly large bodies of water. This, however, was a moat. Memmie's moat. Did I dare?

I excused myself, quickly retrieved my backpack from the car and ducked behind some bushes. I could hear them chatting even more freely in my absence, since I was definitely the weak link in the conversation. Eric and Marie-Ange had questions, but Alec and Ivy knew what I was up to.

I came out from behind the bushes wearing my tank suit and cap.

"Non!" Marie-Ange gasped as she realized what I was about to do. She crossed her arms across her chest. "C'est trop froid!"

"Pas de problem," I reassured her. "Je suis Canadienne!"

I plunged into the moat. It wasn't particularly cold, but it was awfully murky. It was a moat, after all. I estimated it was somewhere in length between twenty-five and fifty meters. I did a quick front crawl to the end and back, aware that we had to get on the road soon. But with its high sides, the moat was harder to get out of than it was to get into. I grabbed onto some nondescript vegetation lining the upper edge and was able to hoist myself up and out of the water. I threw on my towel, planning to change in the car, and we piled in. Just as we were pulling away, Marie-Ange came running from the house carrying a bottle of *champagne rosé* and passed it through the open window. Alec wanted to pay, but they wouldn't hear of it. It was a gift for the woman who had swum in *l'eau de la fille sauvage*.

Swim Home

We arrived at the station, dropped off the rental car, and got to the platform just as the train was about to leave. Back in Paris, we pondered what to do with the sparkling *ros*é. We couldn't take it on the plane – no liquids allowed in carry-on. And we couldn't risk having it explode in our checked baggage. What choice did we have? We'd just have to drink it up tonight.

At one point, I felt a strange sensation on my skin – a surge of pins-and-needles. I kept folding and packing, waiting for it to pass, but instead it grew more and more intense. I started to worry. What was this? Was it dangerous? Should I go to a hospital? It was last thing we needed just hours before our flight home. I kept on drinking the sparkling *rosé*. When the pins-and-needles feeling finally started to subside, I was drunk enough that I'd stopped worrying about it.

I crawled into bed and drifted off into a pleasant stupor, dreaming of my swim in Memmie's moat. In the coming years, I came to realize that our last-minute decision to visit Songy had done more than introduce me to the glories of champagne. It had laid the foundation for all the elements of Memmie's story – both historical and contemporary – that would occupy my attention for the next decade.

CHAPTER 4

The Learned Men and the Secretary

"She herself was so used to the water when she first came to France, she could not live without it, and was used to diving in overhead and ears, and to continue swimming and diving like an otter, or some other amphibious animal. And when they restrained her from this practice, when she was a little tamed and civilized, she thought her health suffered for want of it."

-from the preface to the English translation of Mme. Hecquet's *Histoire d'une Jeune Fille Sauvage* by James Burnett, Lord Monboddo, published in Edinburgh in 1768

Throughout history many human societies have indulged in the practice of swimming, but eighteenth-century France was most definitely not one of them. Plunging into a lake or river stripped down to light underclothing or even – gasp! – completely naked was simply not done. Why would a person want to do such a thing, except, occasionally, to wash off the residue of hard physical labour?

A brief dip for bathing purposes certainly wasn't what drove Memmie LeBlanc into the water. To all accounts she was a vigorous swimmer, who exulted being in water, as the above quote attests. For the Wild Girl, swimming was the most natural thing in the world. Which meant, of course, that the habit had to be bred out of her

– along with the eating of raw meat and climbing trees – and her keepers proceeded to do just that.

Over the past decade I've pondered the roots of my deep sense of kinship with Marie-Angelique, but our shared love of swimming was the jumping-off point. (Her propensity for climbing trees, not so much). I'm a swimmer, too. I *need* to be in water on a regular basis, and not in a pool (though sometimes that's the only option) but a natural body of water. For years I've been swimming daily in Lake Ontario, near where I live on Toronto Island, for as much of the year as I can. For me, water is a physiological and psychology necessity. It keeps me sane. Reading accounts of the tactics used to keep Marie-Angelique out of the water filled me with dread. Barring her from swimming felt to me like a form of torture.

In her own day, the Wild Girl's penchant for the water was one of the main factors in the sensational curiosity she aroused among the general public. But there was a smaller cohort of distinguished intellectuals, "Learned Gentlemen," who attempted to rescue her story from the realm of myth and fairy tale and situate it in a rational, understandable context. Back in the eighteenth century, there weren't practising "scientists" in the way we think of them now. In fact, though the present-day practitioners of hard science are somewhat loath to admit it, the roots of modern science lie in the discipline of philosophy – more specifically, what was known as "natural philosophy." The pioneers of physics and astronomy, Newton and Galileo, both answered to the title of "natural philosopher" in their own time. (The title of Newton's *magnum opus* was *Mathematical Principles of Natural Philosophy*.) And while, like modern scientists, most natural philosophers believed in the primacy of empirical evidence, they didn't have access to the modern system of controlled experiments, which was in its infancy. The boundaries between the various disciplines were more fluid than they are today, freeing these learned men, supported by patrons or their own personal wealth, to follow wherever their eclectic interests led.

Few eighteenth-century figures had greater renown than Charles Marie de la Condamine, the first of the learned gentlemen to investigate the mysterious case of the Wild Girl. In fact, La Condamine was as much an explorer and adventurer as a natural philosopher. He was most famous for his trips to South America, where he spent ten years measuring degrees of latitude and longitude around the equator, led the first scientific exploration of the Amazon, and discovered the use of quinine, an extract of cinchona bark, to cure malaria. He first met Marie-Angelique about ten years after she appeared in Songy. By then she had learned to speak, and only traces of her life in the wild persisted. When he first heard about the Wild Girl, he was skeptical and decided to find out the truth for himself. Through several meetings over the next decade, he concluded that the basic outlines of her story were true. La Condamine was determined to bring a degree of rigour to the investigation, to put an end to the idle speculation: Was she Norwegian? Caribbean? Did she come from a tribe of cannibals? Curiously, he turned over the heavy lifting of this investigative task to a little-known person with no standing in the circle of natural philosophers. And a woman to boot.

Marie-Catherine Homassel Hecquet is one of those people whom history remembers only for her association with someone far more interesting. Her biography of Marie-Angelique LeBlanc, *Histoire d'une Jeune Fille Sauvage Trouvée dans les Bois a l'age de Dix Ans*, published in 1755, was for many years regarded as the definitive account of the Wild Girl's life. And yet Hecquet's contribution to unravelling the mystery of the Wild Girl has been minimized; her role reduced to something like a glorified secretary to La Condamine. Hecquet herself did little to counter this impression. As she wrote in her preface, "This narrative has been drawn up under the immediate inspection of M. de la Condamine, whose curiosity and accuracy in matters of this sort is well known." Even now, speculation persists that Hecquet simply provided a pseudonym for the true author, who was La Condamine himself. Aside from being an example of garden-variety eighteenth-century sexism, it may have had more to do with the fact that the *Histoire* was Hecquet's first book, and the only one published in her lifetime. The imprimatur of someone with La Condamine's status was no doubt crucial to the work being taken seriously.

Whoever conducted the interviews or did the actual writing, the *Histoire d'un Jeune Fille Sauvage* is an impressive piece of work. The range of questions Hecquet posed and her attention to detail go a long way toward making order of the strange saga. She is careful not to gloss over areas of uncertainty and cautions that in some cases Marie-Angelique might be conflating her own memories with details suggested to her by others. Overall, Hecquet succeeds in constructing a plausible narrative, by modern standards as well as those of her own time. The first pages of the book are drawn from the early eyewitness accounts and recount the much-told tales – the killing of the dog, the grabbing and eating of the raw chicken. The book states that early observers were "of the opinion that she was about nine years of age," which, as we'll see, is a detail that became the source of some controversy. The book also documents the Wild Girl's many attempts to escape in the early days after she was discovered. In one, she is found asleep in a tree, on a bitterly cold night, which gives rise to the legend of her extraordinary tolerance for cold temperatures.

From the hearsay of third-person testimony, Hecquet moves on to the findings of her own interviews, in which Marie-Angelique details her vague recollections of her early life, her travels with an unnamed companion, and a harrowing account of being fired upon by a hunter while swimming across the Marne. Trees, Marie-Angelique tells Hecquet, were their refuge from predators, cradling them to sleep at nighttime and providing watchtowers to survey their surroundings from a distance. Before she acquired language, whenever Marie-Angelique was asked about her mother or father, she would point to a tree.

Here is found one of the most striking elements of the Wild Girl's story; an account of her fierce brawl with her unnamed companion arguing over a *chapelet* – a rosary they found on the ground. This event is one of the first incidents Marie-Angelique told Hecquet about, recounting in great detail how she struck the other girl on the head, causing a bleeding wound which she quickly tried to stanch with the skin of a frog. "After this," Hecquet notes with understatement, "they separated."

Here, as elsewhere in the book, Hecquet cautions that Marie-Angelique's recollections may not be completely reliable, due to the passage of time and the fact that she was only able to describe events after she'd learned to express herself in French. But one thing about which Hecquet expresses no doubt is Marie-Angelique's horror of being touched by men. The book recounts a number of incidents in which she shrieks at men who approach too closely, in particular one whose face she slaps with a piece of raw meat, nearly knocking him off his feet. Hecquet speculates this fear might stem from a "dread of ill usage" Marie-Angelique had experienced sometime in the past – a euphemism for what we now call sexual assault.

There is much discussion of Marie-Angelique's health problems, which both she and Hecquet attribute to the forced "taming" and change of diet to which she was subjected. Marie-Angelique tells Hecquet that in one of her convent stays, the nuns refused to let her outside because she wasn't sufficiently cured of her desire to swim and climb trees. In fact, these two activities proved to be the most difficult of her wild habits to shed, which should have been no surprise. For all that her European overlords considered swimming and climbing trees "unseemly in a girl," these activities clearly had been a normal – and enjoyable – part of her previous life.

At their very first meeting, Hecquet notes that Marie-Angelique appears to be in delicate health, and also learns that her financial future is uncertain, due to the death of her long-time patron, the Duc d'Orleans. Hecquet expresses great concern for Marie-Angelique's future well-being, but Marie-Angelique assures her that Divine Providence protected her during her time in the forest and will continue to shield her from harm. Hecquet, a person of devout, even austere piety, is deeply moved by Marie-Angelique's words, taking them as proof that the savage has truly adopted Christianity.

Hecquet continually probes, without much luck, into Marie-Angelique's recollections of her early life. But one memory she summons up turns out to be pivotal: Marie-Angelique tells of an encounter she once had, while swimming, with a "huge animal swimming with two feet, like a dog," with "large, sparkling eyes" and short black hair. Hecquet is certain that the creature is a seal and seizes on this to support her argument that Marie-Angelique "is of the *Esquimaux* nation[2], which inhabits the country of Labrador, lying to the north of Canada." Other details bolster her thesis, such as Marie-Angelique's taste for raw fish and her propensity for diving into cold water. Despite Hecquet's demurrals elsewhere in the book that, given the passage of time, the Wild Girl's memories are "very little to be depended on," the vividness of the seal-image convinces her of the Wild Girl's northern origins.

Hecquet had gleaned a good deal of her knowledge of life in North America from her childhood friend Marie-Andre Regnard Duplessis de Saint-Helene, a nun who emigrated to New France and became Mother Superior at the Hotel-Dieu in Quebec. Though few of Hecquet's letters have been preserved, Duplessis' side of the correspondence contains detailed descriptions of the manners and customs of various native groups. The clincher, for Hecquet at least, was Marie-Angelique's reaction to a collection of Indigenous dolls sent to her by Duplessis. Upon seeing them, Marie-Angelique immediately gravitated to the two figures – a male and a female – in Inuit dress. She told Hecquet they looked familiar, that she was sure she had seen people like them before.

Duplessis' letters certainly suggest that she had more than a passing knowledge of Inuit life, and she gets many details right, such as their practice of eating raw seal and sewing sealskins for garments. Yet Hecquet chooses to quote this excerpt from Duplessis' letter of October 30, 1751: "The Esquimaux are the most savage of savages. Though the manner of the other indigenous nations appears extraordinary, they still retain some tincture of humanity.

---

2 Because discussion of her nationality appears so frequently in both French and English sources, in this book I use the French version of the now-discredited term "Eskimo."

But among the Esquimaux, an almost incredible barbarism universally prevails. They are a nation of Anthropophagi, who devour men whenever they can get them."

Convinced of Marie-Angelique's *Esquimaux* origins, Hecquet proceeds to cobble together a narrative of how the girl might have been brought to Europe, how her ship landed in the Netherlands, and how she and her unnamed companion spent months – perhaps years – making their way through the Ardennes Forest to the Champagne district. She ends the book with several appendices, which include Marie-Angelique's baptismal record of June 16, 1732 and extracts of letters written by witnesses a couple of months after her appearance in Songy. One of the letters states that Marie-Angelique appeared to be about eighteen years old, which Hecquet dismisses as an error. The same letter refers to the Wild Girl's "lively blue eyes" – the sole mention of her eye colour in any of the surviving accounts, and a curious detail in light of the belief that she was an indigenous North American.

The Lawyer-Linguist and the Forbidden Experiment

If Hecquet was overshadowed by La Condamine, the one who really stole her thunder was James Burnett, Lord Monboddo. Like Hecquet, Burnett was introduced to Marie-Angelique by La Condamine and met with her a full decade after the publication of Hecquet's *Histoire*. Burnett was a prominent Scottish lawyer, and a high point of his legal career was his role in the Douglas Cause, a scandalous inheritance dispute involving false identities and a French rope dancer that gripped Europe in the 1760s. But today he's most remembered for his connection to the poet Robert Burns. Smitten with Burnett's daughter Elizabeth, Burns was a frequent houseguest at Monboddo Castle, the family manor near Aberdeen, which still stands today. The poet praised Elizabeth's beauty in several poems and letters and wrote a famous Elegy upon her untimely death at the age of twenty-four.

Kathleen McDonnell

AN ACCOUNT

OF A

SAVAGE GIRL,

CAUGHT WILD in the WOODS of CHAMPAGNE.

TRANSLATED

From the FRENCH of Madam H—T.

WITH

A PREFACE,

Containing several Particulars omitted in the Original Account.

Like many learned gentlemen of the eighteenth-century, Burnett's true interests lay less in his day job and more in natural philosophy, and the new ripples of thought it generated in the European worldview. He took part in the intellectual circles in Edinburgh during the period historians refer to as the Scottish Enlightenment. Burnett carved out a territory for himself in the study of languages and was an early pioneer in the field of linguistics. His *magnum opus,* entitled *On the Origin and Progress of Language,* was published in 1774. He was intrigued by accounts of the Wild Girl and seized upon an opportunity to meet her on a Douglas Cause-related trip to Paris in 1765. With his clerk, William Robertson, serving as translator, Burnett conducted a number of interviews with Marie-Angelique. When he returned to Scotland, he had Robertson translate the *Histoire*, adding a preface that he wrote himself, and he published the English edition in 1778. In the book, Burnett acknowledges his debt to La Condamine and refers to himself in the third person as a "Scotch gentleman of distinction."

When someone writes a preface to a book it's usually to praise it, but Burnett didn't follow the etiquette on that point. In fact, he wasted no time getting around to his main agenda, which was to challenge Hecquet's view that Marie-Angelique was *Esquimaux*. His argument relied on his own area of expertise, linguistics, but he also drew on the findings of his own interviews with Marie-Angelique, which expand upon and in some cases – in his words – "correct" statements in the *Histoire*. His preface mentions only in passing the "hot country" stopover that Marie-Angelique's ship was supposed to have made before sailing to Europe. His greater interest is in the "cold country" from which she came, for on that point he is in agreement with Hecquet. He believed Marie-Angelique indeed came from a northern country, but he is certain that she herself is not of the *Esquimaux* nation. His first line of argument is based on her appearance; she has fair skin and smooth features, unlike the *Esquimaux* who are, "by the accounts of all travellers the ugliest of men, of the harshest and most disagreeable features." (Sounds like he got his information from the same people as Mme. Duplessis.) There's a certain poignance when he talks about the forbidden activities Marie-Angelique found it so hard to give up: In her home country, "the children are accustomed to the water from the moment of birth, and they learn to swim as soon as to walk... They are also taught very early to climb trees; a child of a year old there is able to climb a tree."

Burnett's ace in the hole was his familiarity with North American Indigenous languages. Having established that Marie-Angelique came from what is now Northern Quebec, on the eastern shore of Hudson Bay, he determines that her people were speakers of the

Huron language. From explorers' reports, Burnett had gleaned that Huron speakers had difficulty forming labial consonants, and made many "guttural consonants, with very little use of the tongue and none at all of the lips." These characteristics match up with Marie-Angelique's own memories and his observations of her speech patterns. Burnett says that the use of Huron was "very widespread over all the continent of North America." In fact, like the broader Iroquoian language family of which it is considered a subgroup, Huron was spoken in the Great Lakes region, but probably did not extend as far north as Hudson Bay. So, though Burnett's argument may have been a bit of a stretch, given the state of knowledge and eighteenth-century mapmaking, it's not surprising.

Burnett and Hecquet were asking the same three key questions about Marie-Angelique: Who was she? Where did she come from? How did she end up in the woods in France? They may have arrived at different conclusions, but they both appear to have succumbed to what we now call confirmation bias. Like many who encountered the Wild Girl, Hecquet decided early on that Marie-Angelique was *Esquimaux* and built her case around that. Given that many of her queries were likely what we would consider "leading questions," it's hard not to conclude that Hecquet overplayed her hand. Burnett, who was ostensibly of a more rigorous, empirical bent, nevertheless bent his observations to fit his own linguistic bias.

Burnett had an even broader agenda in studying the Wild Girl. More than a decade after his interviews with Marie-Angelique, he met and studied another, even more famous savage child; Peter the Wild Boy of Hanover, found in the forest in northern Germany in 1725. In his later writings Burnett hypothesized that feral children like Marie-Angelique and Peter might provide science with a glimpse of humankind's original nature; our primitive state before we acquired language. This quest had a long history that predated Burnett and his eighteenth-century colleagues. The most notorious was the attempt by the Emperor Frederick II, in the year 1211, to discover what he called "the natural language of God" – the language that the Deity would, presumably, have imparted unto Adam and Eve in the Garden of Eden. Frederick ordered that a group of newborn babies be taken from their mothers and raised by nurses in an atmosphere of complete silence. The nurses were allowed to feed, bathe, and clothe the children, but forbidden to prattle or communicate with them in any way. The outcome of this experiment was disastrous. None of the babies survived past childhood, and all perished without ever uttering a single word.

The emperor's bizarre venture came to be known as the Forbidden Experiment, and it had come to be considered completely unethical well before Burnett's time. But the desire to observe humans in this "state of nature" persisted and explains much of the abiding fascination for feral children among eighteenth-century thinkers. Here were humans who, having been isolated from human contact from their earliest days, offered an opportunity to observe nature in itself, freed from civilizing influences. Unlike the babies in Frederick's Forbidden Experiment, the situation of feral children had been brought about by happenstance, and so didn't pose the same moral dilemma. (Some of these ethical questions are explored in the fascinating 2018 documentary *Three Identical Strangers*, about triplet infant boys raised apart in a chilling, modern-day version of the Forbidden Experiment.)

Burnett's studies of feral children were part of his lifelong quest to "trace the progress of our species through all its various stages, to mark by what degrees we have passed from the animal to the savage, and from the savage to the civilized man." In this he is considered to be a proto-Darwinist, an early proponent of the notion of evolution. Burnett was one of a number of eighteenth-century natural philosophers who toyed with the idea of evolution, including Darwin's own grandfather, Erasmus Darwin. (Charles Darwin's breakthrough was not the theory of evolution *per se* but the discovery of how it worked, via Natural Selection.) Like many pioneers, Burnett made mistakes, some of which turned out to be howlers. He was mocked mercilessly by contemporaries for his theory that humans had once had tails, and Samuel Johnson ridiculed his idea that orangutans could be taught to speak. The decline of his late-life reputation provided a bit of poetic justice for Hecquet, who is still dismissed by modern-day commentators for her lack of credentials. In the final analysis, both Burnett and Hecquet did the best they could with what they had to work with, and it's fascinating that both of them turned out to be partly right about Marie-Angelique's origins. But it would take another three centuries for the full story to emerge.

CHAPTER 5
The Surgeon and the Scholar

Seule la grande sécheresse de 1731 porte la responsabilité de ta capture. ("It is only the great drought of 1731 that is responsible for your capture.")

-from *Marie-Angelique (Haut-Mississippi, 1712–Paris, 1775)* by Serge Aroles

After devouring these historical accounts, I was hooked. The Wild Girl's story had all the ingredients for a riveting piece of theater; mystery, tragedy, even a touch of romance! Most of my previous work in fiction and theater had been aimed at young readers and audiences, but I felt the sweep of this story called for a more sophisticated approach. I did what writers do at this early stage on the creative process – I jotted down thoughts, scribbled bits of dialogue, and embarked on further reading. But when I looked for contemporary sources about the Wild Girl of Champagne, I found very little – almost nothing, in fact. Which mystified me. How could such a remarkable life story have been lost to history? I realized it was also an opportunity: Since Marie-Angelique's story had so many gaps, these were mine to fill in with my imagination. Through writing about her, I could explore my own hopes, fears, disappointments. I could remake her world in my own image. She would become *my* character.

Given the creative opportunities the material offered, I wasn't surprised to find that a few other writers had gotten there before me.

Australian playwright Hilary Bell's piece, entitled, with utter simplicity, *Memmie Le Blanc*, was first produced in 2007. Bell's narrative follows the eighteenth-century accounts in the locale and other details, but also takes major creative liberties. She creates a fictional character, a widow named Catherine, who takes young Memmie in soon after her appearance in Songy in 1731. Recognizing her innate intelligence, her "humanness," Catherine embarks on a series of well-meaning attempts at taming the Wild Girl, aimed at rendering her fit to participate in civilized society. Memmie is beginning to respond to Catherine's disciplinary program when her life is disrupted by the arrival of another fictional character, an ambitious young doctor, who travels everywhere with a pet orangutan he is trying to tame. Memmie forms a bond with the orangutan and is soon torn between her desire to please her teacher and her natural instincts.

The discontents of becoming "civilized" also permeate French novelist Anne Cayre's *La Fille Sauvage de Songy*, published posthumously in 2013. With its similarly unadorned title, this literary novel adheres to the established facts of the Wild Girl's story much more closely than Bell's play. This was partly because Cayre was able to draw on more recent archival research from France that wasn't available to Bell. But her deeper creative purpose in the novel is to give her character a voice, an inner life that is missing from historic accounts.

My own play went through several drafts over the years. Drawing on insights gained from a workshop and two public readings of the script, I pared down the script from a large-cast *Masterpiece Theatre*-style treatment to what I felt was its essence; a two-character drama in which Marie-Angelique and James Burnett appear as both their younger and older selves. Including one of the learned gentlemen as a character was crucial, I felt, to the kind of piece I wanted to write – one with intellectual heft, which explored how Marie-Angelique was viewed by Enlightenment thinkers.

For as much as Marie-Angelique was written *about*, nowhere in the historical record is there a trace of her own voice. Aside from a few of her signatures on legal documents, there is no there there. Creating an inner life for a character who is, in a real sense, unknowable was the challenge Bell, Cayre, and I all grappled with in writing about the Wild Girl. Though we employed different narrative strategies, we all came from a position of deep sympathy and identification with her predicament. As we strained to imagine how she experienced the brutalizing process of being "tamed" and the damage it caused to her psyche, we naturally filled in the blanks with our own projections and preoccupations. Cayre's novel draws heavily on what she called her own "dreams and fictions" to create a vivid inner life for her character, while I depicted Marie-Angelique's love of water as a longing for the home she had lost all memory of. In one scene, I imagined her trying to "swim home" underneath the bridges over the Seine as it flows toward the sea. Bell and I also chose to explore the philosophical debates that the Wild Girl's story stirred up in Europe. There's an intriguing parallel between the two plays; mine also featured an orangutan – deceased and stuffed, not the living animal of Bell's piece. Both of us drew on the Natural Philosophers' burgeoning interest in primates for the window they hoped to find into human nature itself. But in the writing process, that made it difficult to avoid falling into caricature, to focus on the mythical, Rousseauian figure than the Wild Girl as a real person.

The biggest unknowable is, of course, the earliest period of Marie-Angelique's life. That's why virtually all stories about her – fictional and non-fictional – essentially begin when she emerges from the Songy woods. But who she was *before* she was brought to France seemed destined to remain a mystery. At least that was the case until the arrival of a new sheriff in town, armed with musty archival documents that no one else had unearthed.

The Archive Hunter

Let's recall that the three key questions those duelling eighteenth-century experts – La Condamine, Hecquet, and Burnett – were trying to answer: Who was the Wild Girl? Where did she come from? How did she end up in the woods of France? Late in the first decade of the new millennium, an archive hunter came forward with new findings from that claimed to answer all of those questions and more. His name was already a familiar one in the world of *enfants sauvages*: Serge Aroles. Having declared in his 2004 book *L'Enigme des Enfants-loup* that Marie-Angelique was the only legitimate case of a feral child in human history, Aroles set out to solve the mystery of her origins, to explain how and why Marie-Angelique was able to achieve what no other feral child had – full integration into mainstream society. Scouring through hundreds of archival documents in France and North America, Aroles published his findings in a follow-up book, *Marie-Angelique (Haut-Mississippi, 1712–Paris, 1775): Survie et Résurrection d'une Enfant Perdue Dix Années en Forêt.* ("Marie-Angelique, Upper Mississippi, 1712 – Paris, 1775: Survival and resurrection of a child lost in the forest for ten years.") What Aroles claimed to have uncovered would lead to a major revision of Marie-Angelique's story as a Wild-Child fable. The book announced a definitive answer to the first two key questions, tracing her roots to a particular time and place.

The Fox tribe, also known as the Meskwaki, lived in the Great Lakes region of what was then New France, now the U.S. state of Wisconsin. Aroles' conclusions place Memmie LeBlanc squarely in the thick of one of the defining and brutal events of early Canadian history.

In the late seventeenth and early eighteenth centuries, France engaged in a complex series of alliances with various Indigenous nations, including the Fox or *les Renards*. Though up until 1712 they'd been allies, the French decided that the Fox were a major obstacle to their domination of the fur trade, and they began a decades-long campaign of extermination that historians call the Fox Wars. Though the French forces did not succeed in wiping out the Meskwaki, they tortured and killed thousands of men, women, and children. A small number of survivors escaped New France and eventually settled in present-day Iowa, where the tribe lives and flourishes today. During the hostilities, a large number of Fox adults and children were enslaved by the French. (A significant number of present-day *Quebecois* can trace their ancestry back to those Fox slaves.) Aroles concludes that as a young child, Marie-Angelique was taken into slavery by a prominent family, who took her first to Labrador and then with them when they sailed back to France in 1721.

It is in the context of this bloody conflict that Marie-Angélique and many other young *Renardes* were given to the French as slaves. In 1716 the Fox, their numbers already decimated by the hostilities of the previous years, suffered a massive defeat by the French. The governor, Dubuisson, offered clemency to the survivors, who were mainly women and children. This was most likely at the urging of Jesuit missionaries, who were charged with carrying out the primary goal of the Church, which was to Christianize, rather than exterminate the native people. Therefore, if Aroles' conclusions are correct, an unnamed Fox girl – who would eventually become Marie-Angelique – was put in harm's way by French aggression, then snatched from death by French intercession. The French were thus able to seize Indigenous lands and then, on some occasions, "rescue" the Indigenous people from the consequences of their aggression by a combination of intermarriage, adoption, and enslavement.

To top it all off, Aroles also provided an answer to the third key question: How did Marie-Angelique end up in the woods in France? (Bear with me here, it's complicated.) As one of the Fox survivors spared in 1716, she was given to the household of a prominent family, the de Brouagues. After the death of the patriarch, Pierre-Gratien Martel de Brouague, de Brouague's widow, Marie-Charlotte Charest, married Augustin Le Gardeur de Courtemanche, a soldier who had dealings with the Fox in Great Peace negotiations of 1701. The family moved to Labrador when Augustin was appointed commandant and given land to operate a seal fishery and to trade with the Montagnais Indians. After the death of Augustin in 1717, his stepson, François Martel de Brouague, took over the command of the Labrador post. He brought with him a young female Fox slave, whom he gave to his mother, Marie-Charlotte de Courtemanche (Augustin's widow) in the summer of 1718. When hostilities broke out between the *Esquimaux* and European settlers, resulting in the burning of Fort Ponchartrain in July 1720, Madame de Courtemanche fled with her two daughters and the future Marie-Angélique. According to the manifest of the ship *l'Aventurier*, Mme. de Courtemanche was accompanied by her daughters and an unnamed *sauvagesse*.

At that time, Marseilles was in the throes of an epidemic, the last major outbreak of bubonic plague in Europe. Trapped for several weeks in quarantine and panicked because she had run out of money, Mme. de Courtmanche begged the Court to let her leave Marseilles. A man named Sieur Ollive, who owned a silk factory just north of the city, lent her money. In 1721, as payment, Mme. de Courtemanche was forced to give a slave over to Ollive to work in the silk factory. The next we hear of Madame de Courtemanche is in 1723, when another ship's manifest records that she returned to Labrador with her two daughters, but without the young *sauvagesse*.

Aroles' work also claims to clear up some of the mystery surrounding the mysterious companion mentioned by both Hecquet and Burnett. Aroles thinks this person was probably originally from Sudan or Ethiopia, which provided the vast majority of the black slaves in Europe at the beginning of the eighteenth century. This girl and Marie-Angelique would have met at the same silk factory and run away together, helped in their flight by the fact that they crossed a depopulated Provence, devastated by the plague. They presumably spent years – possibly as much as a decade – living in the forest, subsisting on roots, fish, and animal flesh. During their years together, the two girls had no common language and apparently communicated by gestures and vocalizations. Their joint survival was probably aided by their complementary abilities: The African girl was older and stronger, while her Amerindian origin ensured that Marie-Angélique knew the skills of forest survival.

One of the longtime mysteries surrounding the Wild Girl saga was what became of her African companion. The girl who would become Marie-Angelique was alone when she appeared in the fall of 1731. Aroles believes that she was near starvation brought by on a lengthy drought, and that it was desperation that drove her to seek out human contact again. There were reports from the nearby village of Saint-Martin that a black girl had been shot dead in the days before the Wild Girl emerged from the forest, and for years a rumor circulated that she had murdered her own companion. It wasn't until 1765 that the true perpetrator was revealed by James Burnett, who reported that a local man had confessed to firing on the two girls, convinced they were some kind of monsters.

It's no exaggeration to call Aroles' archival research a game-changer. He basically rewrote the script of Marie-Angelique's life, which had stood as a mystery for almost 300 years. Aroles' evidence shows that the ship the *Adventurier* travelled a considerable distance south along the Atlantic coast of North America before turning toward Europe and docking in Marseilles. This might explain the notion, as Hecquet's book suggests, of a stopover in the Caribbean. His scenario also sheds light on Memmie's much-remarked-on horror of being touched by men. Hecquet certainly remarks on it, but Aroles takes it a few logical steps further and suggests the likelihood that she was raped.

Interestingly enough, though Aroles supports Burnett in finding she was not an Inuit, his account nevertheless confirms that Hecquet was on the right track. Memmie was taken to Labrador with de Brouague when she was very young, likely no older than six. This suggests that she may have spent more of her childhood in Labrador than in the Fox lands in modern-day Wisconsin, which would make her memories from that time more vivid and concrete. So Hecquet's belief that she was *Esquimaux* makes sense.

The biggest change wrought by Aroles' research was in Memmie's perceived age. He claims that she was about nineteen years old when she first appeared in Songy, despite the early reports that put her age at about ten. His explanation is that it stems from a simple transcription error, the replacement of *dix-neuf ans* with *dix ans*, which was then carried over into later reports. He also located her death certificate, confirming that she died in Paris in 1775, and says it contains suggestions that she was a wealthy person of high status.

Aroles presents his conclusions as definitive, but a great deal of mystery still lingers around the Wild Girl. In some ways, the narrative arising from Aroles' research raises more questions than it answers.

There are gaps that, realistically, cannot be filled after nearly three centuries. The Sixty-four Dollar question is still this: Was Marie-Angelique Fox? *Esquimaude*? Or of some other origin entirely? There are documented connections between the de Brouague / de Courtemanche families and the Fox, Inuit, and Montagnais nations. There were several *Esquimaux* domestics in the de Brouague household in Labrador, one of whom is known to history; Acoutsina, the daughter of the Inuit chief Ouibignaro, who served as a translator. Acoutsina is known to have returned to her own people in 1719, so she could not have been the slave taken to France by Mme. de Courtemanche. In his massive work *Dictionary of Slaves and Their Owners in French Canada,* Marcel Trudel lists the slave travelling to Marseilles with Mme. de Courtemanche as an *Esquimaude*. After nearly three centuries, it seems the competing narratives of Hecquet and Burnett are still alive.

For some, the reference to the Wild Girl's blue eyes in Hecquet's book complicates matters, giving rise to speculation that she might have been mixed-race. This is a real possibility, given the prevalence of common-law relationships and marriages between European men and Indigenous women in New France. An Australian journalist, Roger Bourke, posits that her blue eyes (if she indeed had blue eyes) might have been inherited from Viking ancestors who interbred with the long-extinct Beothuk tribe in Newfoundland centuries before Columbus. His theory is not as far-fetched as it sounds. There is some historical evidence, bolstered by Norse legends, that for a period of time around 1,000 AD, Vikings and Beothuks peacefully co-inhabited near the site of present-day l'Anse aux Meadows, and may well have interbred.

For Serge Aroles, however, there is no uncertainty. In his view, Memmie's Fox heritage is an established fact, and it is his narrative that now carries the day. His findings are cited in a number of scholarly publications, and there are abundant references on the Internet to his book *Marie-Angelique (Haut-Mississippi 1712 – Paris 1765)*. I set out to locate a copy of the book so I could view his evidence and see for myself how he arrived at his conclusions. I expected a book in French on a fairly obscure subject would not be easy to track down. What I didn't expect was that it would be impossible.

I discovered that *Marie-Angelique (Haut-Mississippi 1712 – Paris 1765)* was initially self-published by Aroles in a limited printing in 2007. But the book was now out of print and had been for some time. There is no e-book. A worldwide library search in 2017 turned up only a single copy of *Marie-Angelique (Haut-Mississippi 1712 – Paris 1765)* in the *Bibliotheque Nationale de France*. But a subsequent search of the library's own catalogue ends in a "Page not found." Though the book may have been in the collection of the *Bibliotheque Nationale* at one time, that no longer appears to be the case. It gradually dawned on me that many – if not all – of the Internet references were cited by people who'd never actually laid hands on the book, much less read it. Which led to an obvious question. If the book detailing Aroles' extensive archival research and ground-breaking findings about Memmie LeBlanc was impossible to access, how had so many people become convinced by his argument? Was it really true that the mystery of Memmie LeBlanc had, at long last, been solved?

The time-honored path to credibility is to publish research findings so that they can be subjected to scrutiny by scholars and the general public. And indeed, I found some notable scholars of Indigenous history who expressed doubts about Aroles' conclusions. Olive Dickason, a prominent Indigenous historian, made several attempts to find corroborating sources for Aroles' claims, without success. In an online discussion site, Canadian ethnohistorian Charles J. Martijn again raised the question of whether Marie-Angelique was more likely to have been Inuit by birth and said of Aroles' work: "The whole story is inconclusive and strikes me as suspect." Both Dickason and Martijn have passed away in recent years. But the most prominent skeptic is very much alive, and she initially welcomed Aroles' findings and publicly thanked him for sharing them. But when I contacted Julia Viglione Douthwaite, then a professor of French literature at the University of Notre Dame in South Bend, Indiana, the saga took yet another bizarre turn.

A Case of Mistaken Identity

One of the few contemporary writers to explore this unique life story in English, Douthwaite (who recently adopted Viglione as her official surname) has written several books and academic articles on various aspects of the Enlightenment and the French Revolution. But a keen interest in feral children – Marie-Angelique LeBlanc in particular – has also been a theme running through her academic career. Douthwaite published her first scholarly paper on Marie-Angelique in the mid-nineties. "Rewriting the Savage: The extraordinary fictions of the Wild Girl of Champagne" is a wide-ranging exploration of how Marie-Angelique was viewed by eighteenth-century Europeans, as a creature on the boundaries of civilization, a source of shock and entertainment for cultivated people. "The Wild Girl of Champagne… challenged – and threatened – the primacy of a culture that prided itself on rationality and refined, orderly living." The early accounts sensationalized her unruly behaviours, in particular her preference for raw meat, which was seen as a violation of the boundary between human and animal. After her capture she was subjected to a convent education that embraced the tenets of female socialization – "silence, immobility, physical constraint and social surveillance" – which took a terrible toll on her psyche and physical health. Catholicism, in Douthwaite's view, taught Memmie a new sensation; shame and self-loathing. Douthwaite also examines the keen attention that the Wild Girl drew from the intelligentsia of the day; Linnaeus, who included her in his *Systema Naturae* as a sub-species of humans he termed *Puella Campanica*; and Lord Monboddo, who proposed her as representative of a stage of human evolution through time and compared her with the orangutan.

Douthwaite's 2002 book *The Wild Girl, Natural Man and the Monster: Dangerous Experiments in the Age of Enlightenment*, revisited and expanded on the themes she'd explored in her earlier paper. The chapter entitled "Marie-Angelique LeBlanc: Monstrous Femininity" examines the Wild Girl phenomenon through a specifically feminist lens. In a fascinating exploration of female socialization in eighteenth-century France, Douthwaite discusses how differently Marie-Angelique was viewed from male feral children such as Victor of Aveyron and Peter of Hanover, and how she posed a profound threat to the reigning views of proper female conduct of the time. Douthwaite surveys the writings of some of the other learned men who observed Marie-Angelique – in particular the poet, Louis Racine, and the philosopher, Julien Offray de La Mettrie – and shows how they help promulgate the titillating false narratives about her; that that she craved the taste of human blood, that she had murdered – and eaten! – her African companion. This strain of sensationalism continued into the early nineteenth-century, in chapbooks published in England and Scotland, with long-winded titles like: *The Surprising Savage Girl, caught wild in the woods of Champagne, a province of France; Containing a true and faithful narrative of many curious and interesting particulars respecting this wonderful Creature.*

Before Serge Aroles came on the scene, it was Douthwaite's work that put Memmie LeBlanc on the contemporary intellectual map. Douthwaite's main focus has been on the Wild Girl as a historical and cultural phenomenon and on how she illuminated the times in which she lived. Like most of the rest of the world, Douthwaite was under the impression that the truth of the Wild Girl's origins were a longstanding mystery and destined to remain so. But while working on *The Wild Girl, Natural Man and the Monster* she became aware of some new findings about Marie-Angelique. In her endnotes Douthwaite notes that Marie-Angelique "may have been born a Sioux from the Wisconsin region, bought by a French woman, and transported with her to Labrador then France." This new information arrived as a stream of photos of archival documents, sent to Douthwaite unbidden and out of the blue, by a certain Franck Rolin, whom she acknowledges in footnotes to the book. Franck Rolin, let's recall, was the mysterious Wild Girl enthusiast that the *vigneron* Eric Phelizon had insisted I must talk to back in 2009.

A few years after *The Wild Girl, Natural Man and the Monster* was published, Douthwaite received a copy of Serge Aroles' book *Marie-Angelique (Haut-Mississippi 1712 – Paris 1765)* in the mail. She was immediately struck by the coincidence of two contemporary French researchers working on the same subject, each apparently unbeknownst to the other. Or she wondered if, perhaps, Serge Aroles might be a student of her earlier source, Franck Rolin? She wrote emails to both men, inquiring if the one had by chance ever encountered the other, and if they were aware of their overlapping interests.

Unlike the mystery of Memmie LeBlanc, this one was soon resolved definitively: "Serge Aroles," turned out to be a pseudonym – for none other than Franck Rolin! Aroles and Rolin, Douthwaite discovered, were one and the same person. To her consternation, her inquiry about their connection led to a testy (to put it mildly) correspondence, which ultimately concluded with her blocking his emails from her inbox. Aroles' chief accusation against Douthwaite was that she had used his research without attributing it to him – this despite the fact that she thanks Franck Rolin and cites him in several footnotes in *The Wild Girl, Natural Man and the Monster*. Rolin / Aroles also claimed that Douthwaite had altered the Wikipedia entry on Marie-Angelique – a bizarre accusation, since she had every right to do so. The very essence of Wikipedia is that it is crowd-sourced and edited by users. In her most recent article, Douthwaite treats Aroles' archival findings about Marie-Angelique with interest and respect but takes issue with his contention that Marie-Angelique's Meskwaki origins are a proven fact. But I'm getting a bit ahead of myself. As we'll see, this was only one of the tempestuous relationships swirling around in the Wild Girl of Champagne saga.

CHAPTER 6

The Librarian, the Mayor, and the Vigneron

"A small child cast adrift on the shores of an unknown continent, a Robinson Crusoe in reverse; a 'savage' alone and isolated in the midst of civilized Europe; a philosopher's conundrum; a wonder to royalty; an inspiration to the pious – Memmie had been all of these."

-from *Savage Girls and Wild Boys: A History of Feral Children* by Michael Newton

January 2017: I'm standing in a large, light-filled room in the Bibliotheque Georges Pompidou in the city of Chalons-en-Champagne, France. Three of the four walls are glass, full windows looking over the small plaza at the entrance to the *bibliotheque*. Around me are about a dozen hanging banners dotted with illustrations and text, and several display cases containing very old books and other documents. It's all part of a newly-mounted exhibit entitled "*Sauvage*," an *Exposition*, as the French call it, documenting the life and times of Marie-Angelique LeBlanc, the woman variously known as the *La Fille Sauvage*, the Maid of Chalons, the Wild Girl of Champagne, and other folkloric-sounding names. It's basically Everything You Ever Wanted to Know about Memmie LeBlanc, and quite a few things you didn't even know you wanted to know.

Chalons-en-Champagne is, as its name suggests, a city (of about 45,000 people) in the Champagne district of France. Over the traffic circle in the centre of town looms the statue of city's most famous son, Jean Talon, the first governor or *intendant* of New France in 1670. (Latter-day Canadians are mostly acquainted with Jean Talon as the namesake of Montreal's celebrated outdoor market.) Like so much of Europe, Chalons-en-Champagne has centuries of its history still visible in its structures and, especially, its churches. The old-town section of the city is charming, dotted with eighteenth-century low-rise buildings of timber and clay with exposed-beam facades. But other than the excellent, small-producer namesake beverages available in every restaurant, café, and grocery in town, there isn't much else to distinguish the place from the hundreds of other small-to-medium towns that dot this part of the country.

Like the rest of this economically depressed region, Chalons has seen a steady drop in population over the past two decades, and its main street is full of boarded-up storefronts. That's a big part of the reality that the *Exposition* is aimed at correcting – to promote tourism, to make the city more than a point on the map. The city is about a twenty-minute drive from Songy, but it arguably has an even deeper connection to the Wild Girl, who lived here intermittently in the years following her emergence from the woods. The *Exposition* appears to be a success. Several dozen *Challonnais* attend the opening, expressing surprise and delight that such a remarkable story is part of their local history. Yet for many, this is the first time they've heard about *la Fille Sauvage* and her connection to the area.

The roots of the *Exposition* go back more than a decade, when librarian Isabelle Guyot received a request from an English researcher for information about the Wild Girl. She had only a vague knowledge of the story herself, so to answer the query, she delved into the municipal archives and found… almost nothing. "I was surprised at how little known she was, right here in the area where it had taken place." Around the same time, her son told her about an episode of a sci-fi TV series whose storyline revolved around a feral child. A character in the episode makes a passing mention of Marie-Angelique as one of the notable wild children in history. Guyot was struck by the fact that the Wild Girl appeared to be better known outside France rather than where the story had actually taken place – a situation she resolved to correct.

It was some months before Guyot began her research in earnest, prompted by a life-altering cancer diagnosis. Her treatment and recovery necessitated taking a sick leave, which ended up lasting a full year, and this gave her time to focus completely on Marie-Angelique. She made the most of it, tracking down sources and combing the web for bits of information. When she returned to work, she approached Pierre Gandil, director of heritage collections at the *bibliotheque*, with the idea for an *exposition*. They spent the next few years pulling the pieces together from various sources. Several years into the task, they learned that they weren't the only ones committed to telling the world about the Wild Girl's remarkable saga.

Early 2015 saw the publication in France of a *bande dessinée* or BD about Marie-Angelique, entitled *Sauvage*. BD is the commonly-used French term for a comic book, but *Sauvage*, a hardcover, heavily illustrated book of more than 200 pages, is closer to what is known in English as a graphic novel. A collaboration between artist Gaëlle Hersent and writers Aurélie Bévière and Jean-David Morvan, *Sauvage* is subtitled a "biography" of Marie-Angelique LeBlanc and gives an illustrated account of her life from her birth in North America to her death in France. Serge Aroles is credited on the title page of the BD and *Sauvage* is largely derived from his research. But the creators make clear in an endnote that the result is "NOTRE [sic] vision de Marie-Angelique," and have felt free to employ some degree of artistic license in telling the story. For instance, they give the child who will become Marie-Angelique a name, Mahwewa, though her actual birth name is not known and likely never will be. (*Mahwewa* means "wolf" in the Meskwaki language. Wolves always seem to enter the picture one way or another in stories about feral children.) They've also clearly drawn on anthropological sources for indigenous folk wisdom. For example, a midwife warns Mahwewa's mother about various pregnancy taboos: "Don't look in the left eye of a cadaver or your baby will have a squint." More problematic was the BD's cover, which depicted the *Fille Sauvage* sitting by a stream, chowing down on a live frog with blood streaming from her lips. The image caused some controversy in France. Even though it's based on the eyewitness accounts of her behavior in Songy, many found the cover repugnant. For me, a more fundamental concern is that it reinforces the centuries-old European stereotype of Indians as beast-like creatures. I very much doubt the same cover would pass muster in the current North American socio-political climate.

Even with the cover controversy, the BD was well-received by cultural critics and the French public. Its success prompted Guyot and Gandil to join forces with Hersent, whose illustrations for the BD provided an overall visual identity for the *Exposition*. As I walked through the displays in the *Bibliotheque* Pompidou, I began to comprehend the true impact of their collaboration. Here are the various houses and convents she'd lived in; here are documents signed in her own hand; here is the inventory of items in her apartment after her death in 1775, which suggests that she may well have been a person of some wealth and stature. The real achievement of the *Exposition*, above all, lies in its portrait of the Wild Girl as a real person, rather than a figure of folklore. After nearly 300 years, Marie-Angelique LeBlanc is finally retaking her place in history.

And yet I had to admit that this complicated things for me and my play, which I'd based on the idea that Marie-Angelique was poor and that her ultimate fate was unknown. She had been "my" character, a blank slate on which I could draw with creative freedom. But now there were new, verifiable facts to consider. Until recently the Wild Girl was thought to have been lost to history. Now that she was found, I wasn't at all sure I wanted to bow to the needs of historical accuracy. Like Bell, Cayre, and the BD authors, I wanted to stay true to "MY vision." Yet even before the *Exposition* at Chalons, the play had been in limbo for some time. People were fascinated with the story, and I'd gotten encouraging feedback from theatres on the script, which had been chosen as a finalist in the respected Kentucky Women Writers' Playwriting competition.

But something wasn't right. I knew there was some strong writing in my script, but the whole hadn't jelled. I never felt it was finished, and for some reason, I couldn't fully get behind it. I couldn't put my finger on what the problem was, and I didn't know how to fix it. So, I put the play aside and moved on to other projects. (I'd say the script languished in a drawer, except nowadays we're talking about documents sitting on the hard drive of a laptop.) This is what writers do when a work-in-progress goes stale – put it aside and wait to see if something happens to bring you back to it.

Black Nuns and Iron Masks
Which is exactly what happened to me. It arrived in the fall of 2016, in the form of an email:

> *Dear Kathleen. Would you accept to give a conference talk during the forthcoming exhibition dedicated to Marie-Angélique (an important exhibition, with many original archives documents, books, comic strips, etc.; Châlons, January-March 2017)? They have asked me, but I will be in Ethiopia at this time. Please respond to this email as soon as possible.*

At first, I wasn't sure how to respond. I'd put the play aside, but I hadn't lost interest in Memmie LeBlanc. My obsession with her was stronger than ever. But go to France to make a presentation? What would I talk about? I couldn't read from the script – the play was written in English, unlikely to garner any interest from French theatres. The email stressed that though the exhibition was being sponsored by the city of Chalons, I would not be paid, and there was not even any money to cover my expenses. I could apply for a travel grant from the Canada Council for the Arts, but if it was turned down, was I prepared to pay my own way? I had to ask myself, was there anything in this for me?

Then there was the intriguing identity of the sender to consider... none other than Franck Rolin, aka Serge Aroles.

This actually wasn't the first time I had heard from him. A year or so earlier I'd received a note via the contact form on my website:

> *Dear Madam McDonnell. There has been several short plays (theatre, radio, etc.) inspired by the life of Marie-Angélique Memmie, without the slightest verification in the archival sources. She was 19 years old, and not 10 years, as you can read it in books using third-hand printed publications. At least, check the Wikipedia French page. ALL MY BEST WISHES FOR YOUR PLAY*

I was surprised that Franck Rolin even knew who I was, since my play hadn't been published, and had had only a couple of public readings in Toronto. It was clear from his email that he was under the impression that my script followed the old thinking about her age, i.e., that the character of Memmie was a child of about ten when she was discovered in Songy, not nineteen as he maintained. This actually wasn't the case at all. From my very earliest drafts, I had envisioned Memmie as at least a teenager; depicting her as a grown woman rather than a child actually suited my artistic purposes better. But, as I came to learn, the question of age was a detail that Rolin was very insistent upon.

When the email inviting me to the *Exposition* arrived, I found other things bewildering as well. Since he seemed to think that I was one of those writers who deviated from his narrative about Memmie, why invite me? In a later email, he assured me that in his view, "artists are free" to depart from the facts, but he certainly appeared to spend a good deal of his time sending corrective e-mails to anyone who continued to propagate the original error about her age. And Ethiopia? Why was he going there? His archival research had basically rewritten the narrative of Wild Girl studies. What could be keeping him from attending the *Exposition* in person?

I turned, of course, to the Internet, which only compounded my confusion. From Wikipedia I learned that Franck Rolin aka Serge Aroles was a medical doctor, a trained surgeon, and an author of research papers combining history and medicine. His doctoral thesis was the only work in French devoted to brain and nerve diseases of the *Esquimaux* from the tenth to the nineteenth centuries. For that he was awarded the Faculty of Medicine Paris V Silver Medal in 1995. Much of the Wikipedia entry was devoted to his writings about feral children and Marie-Angelique in particular. But it was clear that he entertained other lofty preoccupations as well. Most recently he appeared to have spent a good deal of time in the Vatican Secret Archives, digging up stuff about historical figures like the Man in the Iron Mask.

Just to be clear, there really is an entity called the Secret Vatican Archives, which have long been the subject of rumors that they contain evidence of extraterrestrials and demons hiding in the catacombs. The truth is more prosaic and stems from a mistranslation of Latin. The formal name is *Archivum Secretum Apostolicum Vaticanum*. But the word *secretum* is more accurately translated to mean "private" rather than "secret," and the archives contain the personal letters and historic records of popes over the past four centuries. Scholars can view the archives with an introductory letter from a recognized historian or research institute. But overall, access is tightly controlled – not because of visitors from outer space, but because there are documents that, for its own reasons, the Vatican prefers to keep hidden from the public eye.

One of the subjects that Rolin / Aroles researched in the Vatican Archives was a seventeenth-century figure, Louise Marie-Thérèse, known as the Black Nun or "Mooress" of Moret. She was a Benedictine nun whom some believed to be the offspring of King Louis XIV's wife, Marie Theresa, and an African servant with whom she'd had an affair. The plot thickens, though, with the emergence of an alternate theory that the Black Nun was instead the daughter of King Louis XIV himself, the product of HIS illicit affair with a black female servant. That is, unless you buy into the other alternate theory that the mother of the black nun was an actress brought from Africa to play the role of a "savage" in a theatrical production at Versailles…

There's a further twist in this saga, and it's a real doozy: There's a male child as well, possibly a son of Louis XIV and potential heir to the throne, who for unexplained reasons was hidden away in prison for most of his adult life. This is the mysterious figure known as the Man in the Iron Mask, the subject of a 1998 film starring Leonardo DiCaprio. Unfortunately, there are dozens of other candidates for being the masked prisoner. One theory holds that he was a lowly valet implicated in a political scandal, but he's also been identified as a debauched nobleman, a failed assassin, and even the twin brother of Louis XIV.

On Aroles' own website I was able to ascertain his Ethiopian connection. He unearthed documents pertaining to Zaga Christ, another figure from the seventeenth-century, who claimed to be the son and rightful heir of Yaqob, the Emperor of Ethiopia. Zaga Christ lived most of his life in Europe and his main claim to fame seems to have been his tortured romance with a Franciscan nun, Caterina Massimi, with whom he exchanged love letters written in – I kid you not – his own blood. There's a smattering of other subjects, including the controversies about the deaths of the philosopher Diderot and several famous actors in seventeenth-century France. The overall impression left by Aroles' website is somewhat akin to a patchwork quilt. There doesn't appear to be any unifying principle to his interests, other than his penchant for rooting around in centuries-old archives, especially ones exuding a whiff of conspiracy.

And then there was the French Wikipedia entry on Marie-Angelique, where I discovered a whole new twist on Aroles' core subject; his poisoning hypothesis. Aroles claimed to have uncovered evidence that Marie-Angelique did not die a natural death – that she may have been murdered by poisoning. The alleged perpetrator was a known criminal, a man who had borrowed a substantial sum of money from her. When the payment came due, the man, Sieur Goisot, was apparently still in financial straits. Based on evidence that Goisot's own daughter worked at an apothecary and was in Marie-Angelique's house on the morning of her death, Aroles speculates that Goisot might have sent his daughter to poison Marie-Angelique, to avoid paying back the loan. Aroles admits there is no definitive proof for this scenario, but…

I was starting to hear the theme music from *The Twilight Zone* in my head. Just who was this Rolin /Aroles character? A conspiracy theorist? A crackpot? Was the debunker-in-chief of hoaxes himself perpetrating a hoax?

Should I stay or should I go?

Who was I kidding? The simple truth was, I couldn't NOT go. I swallowed hard and wrote back:

"Dear M. Rolin. Thanks for your invitation. Yes, I am very interested in participating."

My acceptance was followed by a flurry of emails – some to me, but mostly ones to the organizers, on which I was copied alongside a long list of other people. Reading through them I realized that Rolin saying he'd been "asked to attend" the *Exposition* had been an understatement. It was obvious that he was heavily involved in every aspect of the event, sending batches of archival document photos with explanations and instructions on their display, commenting on the publicity materials, and suggesting names of important people to contact for support. The emails also gave a window into his embattled mentality, especially his constant preoccupation with those who, in his words, "pillage" his work and take credit for it. In one email he takes aim at an unnamed Wikipedia contributor, "who, in all contempt of me, says that it was Julia Douthwaite who did the first serious work. It is me, Franck Rolin, aka Serge Aroles, who sent Julia Douthwaite, as early as 1996, dozens of unknown major archives on Marie-Angélique. Anglo-American authors who have not seen the archives, are still spreading this mistake, accusing me to be a liar or a 'speculator.' I announce that, after twenty years of indifference, I complain now against anyone looting or assaulting me."

It was my first inkling of his resentment of Douthwaite, the scholar who had become his unwitting nemesis.

I was about to become part of the Serge Aroles universe. Just what had I gotten myself into? I swallowed hard and booked a flight to Paris.

Return to Songy

After grazing the western city limits, the Marne river runs southward from Chalons-en-Champagne. From time to time it was visible from the car, since the highway snakes along the same path. It had been over seven years since I'd been in this part of France, and the familiar landscape of grain fields and vineyards had since become dotted with wind turbines, or *éoliennes* as the French call them. We were heading to the launch of another mounting of the *Exposition* in the village of Songy; ground zero in the saga of the Wild Girl.

The event at the Bibliotheque Pompidou was a success, and my presentation had come off reasonably well, despite my mostly atrocious *prononciation*. (Trust me on this – there is no greater humiliation than speaking poor French to an audience of French people.) I spoke briefly about how I'd first become familiar with Marie-Angelique's story and its connection to Canadian history and then read an excerpt from the play that I'd translated, with expert help, into French. It was a monologue in which Memmie recounts an early attempt to escape from the convent, only to find that civilization has already done its damage:

> "It had been so long since I had run freely. I felt as if my body had been jolted out of a long sleep. I ran and ran, revelling in the air and the blue sky and the sight of clouds over my head. I ran to the river and plunged in. I felt the water wash over me, envelop me. I felt free. I became myself again. I had been apart from life and now I was immersed in it. I resolved at that moment not to go back to that prison. I knew that if I

had to live without running, without swimming, I would die all over again.

"But then the night came on, the sky began to grow dark, and a terrible fear came over me. I had spent countless nights in the forest, and my worst fear was of boars, wolves, creatures that might attack me. But the fear I felt that night was something I had never known before, a nameless terror had me in its grip and would not let go. As the sun came up, my fear lessened. I was hungry, having eaten nothing for nearly a whole day. I spied a plant that I had eaten many times. I dug up the root and began to eat it. But something had changed. It made me feel ill, so I spat it out. I spent the day roaming, looking for something else to eat. I tried to catch a rabbit, some frogs, but I could not. My ears and eyes had become dulled. I had lost the sharpness of mind and senses, the very skills I needed to survive. As the sun dropped low in the sky, I could feel the terror creeping back into my soul. I knew I could not bear to spend another night alone in the forest. I felt that to go back into that nameless fear, that feeling of wanting to scream, and not being able to, would be worse than being torn apart by a wild boar.

"So, I made my way back to the convent. I thought that perhaps I could make the sisters understand, that if only they would allow me to swim from time to time, that would be enough. I wanted to say to them: 'I will stop climbing trees, I will not hunt animals, I promise you! Only let me swim. Please. Do not take that away from me.' But I did not have the words.

"I became resigned to my fate. From the meekness with which I submitted to my punishment the sisters could see that something in me had changed. In time they let me go free for longer and longer periods, until they decided that I no longer needed to be restrained. Even though my body was now free, my mind had become imprisoned. I had lost the urge to run, to eat frogs, even to swim. I had become one who thinks, rather than one who acts. I had become my own captor."

I wasn't at all sure the monologue would make sense separate from the rest of the play. But Pierre Gandil served as translator for the discussion afterwards, and the audience was attentive and gracious. I could feel their appreciation that someone from abroad, far from their little corner of France, shared their fascination with this obscure, centuries-old story.

As expected, Franck Rolin wasn't there, at least not in the flesh. But his presence loomed large over the event. I had already seen from the emails just how hands-on he'd been in the planning. Speaking with Isabelle and Pierre I got a sense of how trying the process had been for them, and I learned from Gaëlle Hersent, the illustrator of *Sauvage*, that the process of creating the BD had been similarly fraught. I found that surprising since the BD hews closely to Rolin's narrative in almost every respect. Nevertheless, the relationship eventually went sour, chiefly over a contract dispute. Rolin insisted on what are known in the publishing world as "subsidiary rights," meaning that the authors and their publisher, Delacorte, cannot pursue adaptations of the BD for other media – television, film, theatre – without his permission, and that he be paid a percentage of the profit from these rights, (which he said would be donated to the people of Ethiopia).

I had been looking forward to the event in Songy, which would give Alec and me an opportunity to renew our acquaintance with the champagne winemakers, Eric and Marie-Ange Phelizon. And at first glance, Songy appeared to be exactly as I remembered it – a quiet, unassuming, eternally unchanging village. But as we drove past the twelfth-century church I noticed that two sides of the building were covered in scaffolding, and that extensive restoration work was going on. And a few other things had changed since 2009. The Phelizon winery now had a prominent sign, and the roofs of the various buildings on the grounds were covered with solar panels. Most thrilling for me – the moat was still there, even longer and wider! I got out of the car and scurried over to the edge of the moat, glad that I'd thought to wear my swimsuit under my clothes. I looked for a spot where I could easily slip into the water (and avoid contact with rash-causing vegetation). It was early spring and colder than when we'd last been here seven years ago. But this time Marie-Ange was well aware of my tolerance for *l'eau froide* and cheered me on.

Later the Phelizons served us a fine, simple meal accompanied by their lovely champagne. Nothing could measure up to the delight of discovery I'd experienced at our earlier visit, though the sparkling rosé Marie-Ange poured came pretty close. But over dinner, we began to pick up indications that all was not wine and roses in the land of *La Fille Sauvage*. It turned out that, completely unbeknownst to us, there had been a struggle between the Phelizons and Francis Passinhas, the mayor of Songy, over who would host us. We'd met the mayor at the *Exposition* in Chalons, where he invited us to come stay at his place, which we of course accepted. We then got in touch with the Phelizons to let them know our plans and that we hoped to see them while we were in Songy. Now we laughed as we told Eric and Marie-Ange how flattered we were to be fought over as guests.

But from their point of view, it was no laughing matter. The mayor's wishes had prevailed, and clearly not for the first time. We were staying at his house and this dinner, *chez* Phelizon, was the consolation prize. Our visit was just another round in a long-running rivalry between *le vigneron* and *le maire,* who, in the time-honored tradition of small-town spats, lived right across the street from each other. Their rivalry had a history, but the present focus of their mutual antagonism was – surprise, surprise – the Wild Girl and her relationship to the town. More than just a personal dispute, this was a true clash of life philosophies.

The majority of residents in Songy have lived their whole lives in the village, but Francis Passinhas was a relative newcomer. Born in Portugal, his family had come to France with the great wave of Portuguese immigration in the 1970s. Passinhas achieved a degree in engineering, settled with his family in Songy, and got involved in local politics. He won his first run at the mayoralty, defeating the previous incumbent, who was none other than the Phelizons' son Flavien. Even from our short stay at his house, I could tell Passinhas was a get-it-done kind of guy, and that his outsider status was a plus in that regard. While the long-time residents see Songy the way it's "always" been, he was constantly thinking about the town's future. He'd managed to raise funds for the restoration of the town's 900-year-old Church of St. Maurice and get it designated a national historical monument. For Passinhas, the Wild Girl's story is the kind of intriguing local history that can build tourism in the area and help restore it to financial health. To him, capitalizing on economic opportunities for the village is his main job as mayor.

Eric Phelizon's attitude toward Marie-Angelique is altogether more complicated. He's not above playing up her connection to his winery; he often recounts the story to customers, telling them they're in a place of historic significance. But the force that really drives him is personal and comes from his deep roots in the area. He dates his ancestors' ownership of the estate back to the first half of the nineteenth-century and says he can't remember a time when he didn't know about the Wild Girl. The story gripped his imagination as a child, not in the way of the bogeyman of local tradition ("If you're naughty, *La Fille Sauvage* will get you!"), but as a source of awe and admiration. His bond with her is rooted in the physical landscape; the fact that he has a day-by-day, hands-on relationship with the place where she lived centuries ago. To Phelizon, it's all well and good that writers and librarians are fascinated with her, but "I am the only one on the ground, working the land she walked on." His attitude is not unlike Rolin's contention that since *he* is the one who searched the archives, it is his view of the Wild Girl that is the correct one. Both men are extreme in their respective beliefs, that the only thing that truly matters is *authenticity*, at least their definition of it. No wonder the *vigneron* and the practical-minded *maire* are like oil and water.

As we prepared to leave Songy, we walked across the Phelizons' field to a spot where a small tributary of the Marne river widens out into a pond. In the middle of the pond is an oval-shaped mound of earth, with a single tree at one end. According to local legend, this spot is known as *l'Ile de la Fille Sauvage* and served as the Wild Girl's occasional refuge from the stresses of civilization for the few months she lived at the D'Epinoy estate. It's a small mound that barely warrants being called an island, and no one knows for sure what the terrain was like in the early eighteenth-century. But even with the modern intrusion of a green plastic bucket sitting on the ground, the place is haunting. The main *chateau* was torn down in the nineteenth century, with only the workers' quarters left standing from the 1700s. This little *ile* is the one place in the village of which we can say for sure, "Marie-Angelique was here."

I feel torn by this small-town rivalry, sad that this remarkable woman's story has been reduced to a local tug-of-war. It's perfectly clear that the best thing would be for the two of them to bury the hatchet and work together. But ownership of this story seems to be the subject of unending struggles. Where the Wild Girl aka *La Fille Sauvage* aka Marie-Angelique Memmie LeBlanc is concerned, nothing is simple.

CHAPTER 7
A Life Like No Other

Ta destinée sera semblable à nulle autre, petite, toutefois la mémoire de l'humanité couronnera si peu ton nom, que l'on doit faire le don de la narration de ton existence à ceux auxquels tu es inconnue. ("Your destiny will be like no other, small, but the memory of humanity will crown your name so little, that one must give the gift of the narration of your existence to those to whom you are unknown.")

-from *Marie-Angelique (Haut-Mississippi, 1712–Paris, 1775)* by Serge Aroles

Back home in Toronto, I expected my experiences at the *Exposition* would kick-start my work on the play, that I'd return to it with fresh insights and enthusiasm. But the opposite happened. I found myself at sea, with no better idea of what to do than when I'd put it aside months before. But, as at so many other turning points in this saga, something in it just wouldn't let go of me. Marie-Angelique, I couldn't quit you.

I decided to embark on a process of mentally uncoupling the real person from the character in my play, starting with her name. Because her birth name is not known, I started thinking of her of as "Little M" and began writing notes, thoughts and, especially, questions that hadn't occurred to me while I was working on the play.

Like every human who ever lived, Little M had a mother. But who was she? What happened to her? Was she enslaved? Did she die giving birth? Or were mother and daughter forced apart later?

In the BD *Sauvage*, Little M's mother gives her to the French to save her from starvation. All of these scenarios are possible, given what's known about the Fox people in the early eighteenth century. However it happened, there's no doubt that in her earliest years, Little M's bond with her mother, with her family and community, was torn asunder. It was a wound that would never truly heal.

I wondered if she might have transferred that mother-bond to her mistress, Mme. de Courtemanche. Maybe it was necessary for her very survival to do so. And so, to an outsider, things might have looked normal, even happy. ("See how fond she is of Madame, and Madame of her.") Maybe Little M. had a few years of happiness with Madame and her children. Maybe she truly did become one of the family; an adopted daughter, not a servant. How keenly she must have felt the hurt, then, when Madame sent her away to work in the silk factory – her, but not Madame's own daughters. They were blood, Little M was not. But who knows? It might have pained Madame greatly to send her away. Maybe she had truly come to love Little M as one of her own. But following Aroles' conclusions from his research, (which is pretty much all we have to go on) Madame had a problem; the debt she owed to Sieur Ollive, the man who had lent her money when she, Little M, and her children were trapped in quarantine. Maybe Madame could see no other way to make it right with her creditor, except to send Little M to work in his silk factory. Madame may have tried her best to explain the situation. She may have told Little M that she would only have to go to the silk factory for a little while. She may have promised Little M that she'd be home soon, and everything would be as it was. Little M must have struggled to understand Madame's words.

What we do know is that Little M was sent away to the silk factory, while Madame's own daughters stayed with their mother. Then in 1723, Madame sailed back to New France, accompanied by her daughters, but without her little *sauvagesse*. Maybe Madame intended to send for her, only to learn she'd run away with another slave. Or did Madame just board the ship and sail away, thinking there was nothing else to be done? That since Little M was not blood, it was best to forget about her?

As I pondered this scenario, I realized there were depths of pathos I hadn't been able to touch on throughout the many drafts of the play. This might have been because I lacked the writing skills, but I was pretty sure it was also the appeal of the "adoption narrative" favored by Europeans. French colonizers told themselves that, by taking Indigenous children into their homes, they were giving them a more materially comfortable (meaning "civilized") life. But even more important was the conviction, reinforced by the Church hierarchy, that they were saving the children's immortal souls by having them baptized into the Catholic faith. This attitude, in different guises, persists right up to our present era. It's only been a few decades since Indigenous children in Canada were forcibly taken from their families and placed in religious-run residential schools. Until relatively recently, it was routine for social agencies to apprehend Indigenous children for adoption into non-Native families. What happened to the girl who would become Marie-Angelique – a child wrenched away from her family, taken to a place far away from everything and everyone she knew – was simply an earlier version of these practices. The idea that she was "adopted" rather than enslaved was a reassuring fantasy, one that I had unwittingly bought into. It opened my eyes to a whole other way of looking at what happened to her.

A Biography like No Other

While all this re-thinking was going on, I was still on the hunt for Serge Aroles' book. Nagged by the areas of uncertainty in his research, I'd tried everything I could think of to locate a copy of *Marie-Angelique (Haut-Mississippi 1712 – Paris 1765)*; Amazon, Google Books, academic sites that specialized in scholarly obscurities. I finally realized I'd have to go straight to the source, and I emailed Franck Rolin, describing my fruitless efforts and asking for advice on how to obtain a copy. I figured that, at the very least, I'd find out why the book – the Rosetta Stone of Wild Girl studies, the linchpin of his archive-hunter reputation – was nowhere to be found. He wrote back promptly, and his response was terse: *Le livre est épuisé depuis longtemps, et je ne me suis jamais soucié de le faire rééditer.* ("The book has been out of print for a long time, and I have never cared to have it reissued.") But Rolin threw in an unexpected curveball with his reply. He mentioned that some years back, he'd sent a copy of the manuscript to an Australian journalist named Roger Bourke.

When Aroles first contacted me in the fall of 2016, it was clear that I was one of several people he was inviting to participate in the *Exposition*. One person copied on the email was Bourke, a writer whose name I'd come across in my online searches about Marie-Angelique. I'd found many references to a website Bourke maintained, *www.marie-angelique.com*. But every time I clicked on the link, the standard Google 404 Error notice popped up, "Page Not Found." Great, I thought, yet another source that had vanished into thin air, and I forgot about it. But Aroles' response brought Bourke back onto my radar. I sent him an email.

He responded quickly, and we embarked on a cordial correspondence about our shared obsession with the Wild Girl. He explained that he'd let the marie-angelique.com website lapse but was working on his own book about her. We exchanged some thoughts and leads, and I told him I was trying to track down a copy of Aroles' book. As it turned out, he did indeed have a copy of the pre-publication manuscript and offered to send it as an email attachment. A day or so later it arrived: 140,000 words, *en francais* in an MS Word document.

It was, as the saying goes, a piece of work.

I went straight to the index, where there were many photos of archival documents relating to the life of Marie-Angélique – thirty in all, though in the introduction Aroles stresses there are "hundreds" more. But, other than the baptismal records of some Fox children from 1713, almost none of the documents bore any relation to Marie-Angelique's early life in North America. Clearly, I wasn't going to get anything more definitive about her origins than the information I already had. What was really striking was the text of the book itself.

In his introduction, Aroles describes the book as *"la biographie est gravée à la seconde personne du singulier."* That is, the entire book is written in the second person singular and is addressed to *"Tu,"* Marie-Angelique herself. Which is, to say the least, a highly unusual way to structure a biography. The other thing that struck me as I skimmed through the text, was that for all its 300-plus pages, there is very little detail about Marie-Angelique's actual day-to-day life. Which isn't surprising, given how little is known about her. What was astounding, though, was the way Aroles dealt with that vacuum – by chronicling an abundance of archival information about everything *else* that was going on at the same time; weather, historical events like the death of King Louis XV, references to famous figures like Voltaire, (who may have met her in 1749) and Samuel Johnson, (who mentioned her in passing in one of his later writings).

At one point, Aroles even has the temerity to correct Mme. Hecquet, a person who actually met and spoke with Marie-Angelique in 1754! In the annals of academia *Marie-Angelique (Haut Mississippi 1712 – Paris 1775)* must certainly go down as one of the great oddities of biographical scholarship. What with the sighting of a comet by Dutch astronomers in 1733, the air temperature in Paris on the Feast of the Epiphany in 1755 (4C.), plus several earthquakes (who knew they occurred so often in eighteenth-century France?), Aroles' book may well be the most complete record of weather events in Europe since the early eighteenth-century. In essence, the book reads like a "life and times" biography of a person that is mostly "times" and very little "life."

Still, deep in the thicket of verbiage and weather reports, the basic timeline of Marie-Angelique's life does emerge; how at the age of six she was captured with other Fox children as spoils of war and taken to the household of Martin de Brouague; how she was later given to his mother Marie-Charlotte Legardeur de Courtemanche (*nee* Charest) and taken to her household in Labrador. That household included a slave girl named Acoutsina, who had learned some French and served as translator for the family. The daughter of an Inuit chief, Acoutsina was treated as a member of the household and was particularly close to Mme. de Courtemanche. She is known to have been allowed to return to her family in 1719. But it's her presence and the presence of other Inuit slaves in the French household in Labrador that has fed some of the skepticism about Aroles' claim that Marie-Angelique was Fox. Mme.'s son Martin de Brouague did own some Fox slaves, and he may well have given one of them to his mother. But in this instance, it might be better to lean toward the principle known as Occam's Razor, namely that the simplest explanation is the most likely explanation, that probably the *sauvagesse* who accompanied Mme. and her daughters to France was *Esquimaux*. And yet, Aroles says that "A story like this could not have happened twice; the *sauvagesse* was necessarily Marie-Angelique." In the absence of solid evidence, he *just knows*. Nowhere in academia, not to mention a court of law, can it be argued that Aroles has proven that the *sauvagesse* was Fox, or that she was the same female who emerged from the Champagne forest a decade later. From "she *could have been* Fox," he leaps to "she *must have been* Fox," and he will brook no departure from that conclusion. Shades of her earlier biographer, Mme. Hecquet! Sooner or later, it seems, anyone who tries to solve the mystery of Memmie LeBlanc falls into the trap of confirmation bias.

At points in his book, Aroles tacitly admits that he's on shaky ground, that the veil of uncertainty about the Wild Girl's origins will never go away. In a section entitled, "Chaos of the Registers," he volunteers the information that between the years 1630 and 1740, one in four Native girls were given names that are variants or combinations of "Marie." This comes from baptismal registers, a core source for historians of New France. So, in each case, the girls' names were changed from their birth names to a Christian one, almost always a saint's name, and variations of Mary, the Mother of God were exceedingly common. Their original names, the ones given them by their parents in the Indigenous communities into which they were born, are unknown. Even with centuries-old record keeping, it's impossible to know for certain which of these baptized Native girls – if any – was the one who would become known as Marie-Angelique.

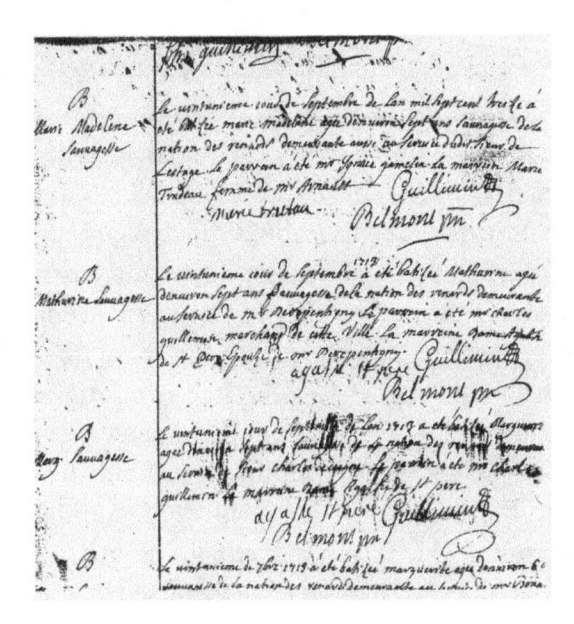

Aroles dates Marie-Angelique's last day in North America as September 11, 1720, the day the family boarded a vessel named, with somewhat mordant irony, the *Adventurer*. After a few stops along the Atlantic coast, they arrived in Marseilles almost six weeks later, to find the port city in the grip of the worst epidemic of bubonic plague since the fourteenth century. Half the city's population had been decimated by the epidemic. After a year stuck in quarantine on the ship, Madame de Courtemanche had run out of money, and sent her little *sauvagesse* to the silk factory. Aroles includes an exhaustive list of various slave ships that arrived in Marseille in 1721, one of which was transporting a girl from Africa who would also be sent to work in Sieur Ollive's silk factory. Aroles believes that she was from Ethiopia and even speculates that she might have been part of that country's royal family. (One suspects he might have wanted to inject a romantic, fairy-tale element into the story.) But whether or not she was of royal lineage, the African girl who escaped with Marie-Angelique must have done so to avoid the terrible fate of life-long enslavement.

Ten Lost Years

It's at this point that a gaping hole emerges in the narrative, one that poses the biggest challenge to Aroles' method. Even he could only fill that empty space with so many earthquakes, eclipses, and royal funerals. From here on, he must draw on Mme. Hecquet's interviews for what little information exists about the two girls' day-to-day survival in the forest. Ten years catching frogs and small animals and eating them raw. Ten seasons sleeping in trees, keeping a lookout, listening for bigger animals who might want to eat them. Ten winters digging holes on cold nights to sleep in, covering themselves with leaves and deadwood to keep warm. The question one really wants to ask is – just *where* were they all that time? The distance between Marseilles and the district of Champagne, where Marie-Angelique finally emerged in 1731, is only about 800 kilometres or 500 miles, an amount of territory they could have traversed in a matter of weeks on foot. At different points in his narrative Aroles situates them in different regions of France, but he offers no historical reports of any sightings that would back him up. Most likely, the two girls were roaming with no particular destination, simply trying to survive – eating when they were hungry if they could find food and sleeping when they were tired if they could find a safe place.

Aroles' medical background is useful in filling in details about what they might have eaten, and how they managed to consume enough nutrients to survive. He suggests, for example, that certain types of vegetation, in particular ferns, would have served as a crucial source of fat and sugar for them. He even conjures up a rather unappetizing picture of Marie-Angelique vomiting up a giant hairball of plant fibres from eating too much grass! He chronicles her adjustment to eating the raw flesh of fish and all manner of rodents and small mammals. Reading his account, I had some questions of my own. Didn't they know how to make a fire for cooking? Was it the fear of being caught that kept them from it? Why didn't they seek help from, say, a farmer? For two girls, one black, one Indian, that question basically answers itself. Didn't it occur to them to seek sanctuary at a church or convent? Perhaps, though they were both already well acquainted with the cruelty Christians were capable of. Unlike the Holocaust survivors I referred to earlier, who fled into the woods where they were fed and sheltered by sympathetic villagers, Marie-Angelique and her African companion had every reason to believe that their survival depended on avoiding contact with other humans.

Marie-Angelique was at least given a name by her captors. The name of her companion is lost to history, and she is remembered only for her connection with the Wild Girl. I had a host of questions about her, too. Aroles claimed that the African girl was older and bigger. Could Marie-Angelique have tried to transfer her mother-bond to the African girl? Was it more of a friend / sibling relationship? Maybe the African girl didn't want to take on the mantle of mother-substitute. Maybe she was annoyed with Little M's attempts to make her into one.

Did they decide to run away together? Or did the African girl plan to escape on her own? Maybe Marie-Angelique tagged along against the African girl's wishes. Maybe they were never close, never bonded. Or maybe, after all those years of living rough, finding food, and staying alive together, how they felt about each other ceased to matter very much. Being two instead of one was an advantage. Each had skills and knowledge the other didn't. The African girl was strong enough to fight off mid-size animals, while Marie-Angelique knew how to catch fish with her hands. In his preface to Hecquet's book, Burnett gives a detailed account of how she once saved the life of the African girl, who could not swim well and held onto Marie-Angelique's foot.

What prompted them to run away? To leave the silk factory, where they at least had food and shelter. Were they escaping a brutal boss? Were they abused, assaulted, raped? (Marie-Angelique admitted as much to Hecquet.) Did they just want their freedom? Did it seem worth the terrible hardship imposed by forest living? Given what's known historically about the slave trade, it was very likely some kind of maltreatment that drove them to run away.

For me, this was another step in uncoupling the character from the real person. It suited my creative purposes to depict my character as completely solitary; as surviving on her own in the woods. But the more I learned from Aroles' work about Madame de Courtemanche's debt to the owner of the silk factory, the more I had to confront the existence of the companion. I found it more and more difficult to avoid concluding that Marie-Angelique was *not* alone. She and the African girl escaped together and roamed the French countryside for a period that might have been as long as ten years. The African girl is mentioned only in passing in the historical accounts because she was already dead by the time Marie-Angelique emerged from the woods. Nothing was known about her. She had no name, no history.

I had my own reasons for writing her out of my version of the story. In his own writing, Aroles appears to fall into a similar trap. For all intents and purposes, he erases the African girl from the day-to-day narrative. The only real object of his interest is Marie-Angelique herself. On occasion, his account acknowledges the other girl's presence, but he rarely depicts the girls in any kind of relationship to one another. The overall effect is as if the African girl is there, but not really there. In what he calls the "decade without speaking" he appears to believe that the two girls had no way of communicating, other than gestures and grunts. But was that really the case? There are numerous examples of humans developing jointly-understood *pidgins* or invented languages in isolated circumstances. Over the years they spent together, it seems highly likely that Marie-Angelique and her companion would have done the same and developed a mode of communication more varied than simple vocalizations.

In truth, the bond between two people who spent a decade in isolation from human society would most surely have been "like no other." I came to realize that my notion of the Wild Girl as a singular, solitary being was a romanticized trope. In fact, she would almost certainly have *not* survived on her own. In her 2013 book *The Village Effect,* psychologist Susan Pinker maintains that face-to-face contact is a human necessity springing from our evolutionary past and hard-wired into our genes. She cites a wealth of medical and social science research to support her argument that the bonds we develop with other humans are as critical to our survival as food and shelter. In Pinker's scheme, it was the girls' companionship, every bit as much as their hunting and fishing skills, that kept them alive in such an extreme situation. Though they'd spent years studiously avoiding contact with other humans, once the African girl was shot dead, Marie-Angelique would likely have found the prospect of life without her intolerable. Perhaps it was a hunger for human contact, not just thirst, that drove her into Songy that September day.

Which is not to suggest that their relationship was an easy one. My guess is that it was akin to a sibling bond, with all the intensity that entails. Aroles was on the right track when he called them "sisters of the woods." Who but siblings would have a knock-down, drag-out, bloody battle over a brightly-colored bauble worn around the neck? Marie-Angelique told Mme. Hecquet that the object they fought over was a rosary, but the event had taken place more than two decades earlier, before she'd been tamed and Christianized. Though as a child she'd lived with a Catholic family, would she really have realized the powerful religious significance of the object after all that time? Was it a rosary at all? She may have said so to bolster her Christian bona-fides with Mme. Hecquet. Because if anything mitigated the public view of her as a savage, it was her oft-stated profession of her Christian faith.

I had other questions about this incident. Marie-Angelique told Hecquet that she and the African girl had parted company over the dispute. But surely it wasn't the first time they'd fought in their many years together. Why the falling-out this time? The only documented sighting of the pair together was by the hunter who ended up killing the African girl. Did Marie-Angelique have survivor guilt? Did she carry thoughts of her long-time companion in her heart for the rest of her days? This, more than anything, is the enduring mystery at the heart of the Wild Girl's story. I was ready to admit that these unknowns gave the story a deeper resonance than anything I could make up.

Twenty Chairs

There were other intriguing threads in Aroles' account, particularly his aforementioned "poisoning hypothesis" and the possibility Marie-Angelique might have had a late-life love affair. The former rests on pieces of evidence that Aroles himself admits are entirely circumstantial. He uncovered documents showing that, in her later years, Marie-Angelique had loaned a considerable sum of money to a Sieur Goisot (ironically, the opposite dilemma that her mistress Madame de Courtemanche had found herself in). But there is no record of this debt being repaid. Sieur Goisot's daughter worked at an apothecary, where she had access to various poison substances. It's noted in Marie-Angelique's death records that the same woman, Goisot's daughter, was present in the house the morning Marie-Angelique died. Aroles speculates that she may have been murdered by Goisot's daughter, who had both opportunity (for procuring poison) and motive (on behalf of her father, who wanted to avoid repaying his debt). Of course, back then establishing a cause of death wasn't the routine process it is today. The doctor who examined the body made no mention of poisoning, and Marie-Angelique was known to have been in poor health for some time. The poisoning hypothesis serves no real purpose other than to add an Agatha Christie-type twist to her passing.

The suitor story has only slightly more substance to it. In her later years, Marie-Angelique had dealings with a man named Pierre-Augustin Hincelot, who may have been a notary. Aroles discovered that a person of the same name lived in Chalons-en-Champagne at the same time as she did. He suggests that this "old friend" sought her out years later in Paris and that their relationship became more than professional, but came to a sad end, likely at Marie-Angelique's urging. It's a fairly meagre foundation for a story of unrequited love, but the appeal of it is understandable. Maybe this woman wasn't just shunned, isolated, and put on display by the society around her. Maybe she was able to establish a true human connection – found someone who loved her for who she was. It's possible, but it could also be a fairy tale meant to assuage European guilt for stealing this woman's life.

A few of the hard facts Aroles uncovered can be found in the inventory of Marie-Angelique's apartment after her death. Among other things, the contents list a total of twenty chairs, which suggest that she was a person of stature who received visitors. Were they visitors she truly welcomed? Were they gawkers who came to see for themselves the refined lady who once ate raw meat? To me, those chairs are a bit like the "second-best bed" Shakespeare left to his wife – so little said, so much implied.

To Aroles, the only kind of information that matters is the kind painstakingly teased out of archives. The most disparaging charge he can muster against his critics is that, unlike him, they have not spent time in the archives and are content to rely on mere "second-hand sources." He does have a point. Primary sources are the gold standard of historical research. Rooting around in archives is painstaking, thankless, exhausting work – hours spent among rows of shelving, rifling through boxes of old documents in obscure, archaic languages. Removing documents from files is seldom allowed – not even for photocopying. (Archival researchers everywhere must say a daily prayer of thanks for the invention of the smartphone camera.) It's a herculean undertaking, requiring people with stubborn, obsessive personalities. And when Aroles refers to "archives" he casts a worldwide net; for his research on Marie-Angelique he searched archival records on both sides of the Atlantic. "I spent a decade in the archives to resuscitate this life, which was like no other. Without my research, all adaptations of her life in these media was impossible, since every notice of her existence began thus: 'Date and place of birth: Unknown. Date and place of death: Unknown.'" He claims that his findings are completely free of self-interest. "I do not explain anything in my book. Nothing. I was not meant to explain anything. Only the evidence of the archives and the narrative form of my text were important to me." But he clearly has a personal investment in the story. "I worked on this biography for myself, not at all for the public, long before the mainstream media became interested in

Marie-Angelique." And his speculations about a doomed love affair and misdeeds surrounding her death could be seen as well-intended efforts to fill in the blanks of a little-known life – to render her more a real person than a mysterious figure of myth.

In places, Aroles' book has a strangely fevered tone that reads almost like a love letter to a woman he never met. In the quote that opens this chapter, I could see my own identification with the Wild Girl writ large. We both share a sense of urgency, a drive to tell the world about her, to restore her to history so she will not be forgotten once again. More than anyone else, Aroles' work situates her in the real world and connects her with an actual time and place and people. Like the Wild Girl's ten years in the forest, he spent a decade buried in archives looking for every scrap of evidence he could lay his hands on about her, and for that we owe him a debt of gratitude.

But it's important to keep in mind that he hasn't really cleared up the mystery of her life. Her pre-European life is the least verifiable of his findings. Where he lacks solid evidence, he writes around the empty spaces and fills in the blanks. Actually, I can relate. There's something that draws all of us – Eric Phelizon, Isabelle Guyot, and Serge Aroles himself – to Marie-Angelique like moths to a flame. Her contemporaries were able to observe and study her first-hand, while we in the modern world are limited to fragments of knowledge gleaned from dusty archival documents. But the passage of time gives us the freedom to imagine and, especially, to *identify* with her profound aloneness, her sense of being a Stranger in a Strange Land. Who among us has not felt like we don't belong?

But the pitfall of this is that we project ourselves onto her, rather than see her for herself. When so much is unknown, the writerly impulse is to imagine what might have been, to build on the known facts and tell the story the way it could possibly have happened. That's what writers do. We bend stories to fit our own purposes and needs. We fill in the gaps. We make stuff up. Which is tempting and easy to do when we're writing about people and events from the distant past. We don't have to deal with the real person, or anyone else who knew her. We're not historians, we're storytellers. Aren't we?

I was beginning to wonder about that.

Even before the *Exposition* I had been feeling some unease about the play, about making this person into a character – "my" character. Seeing the detailed history laid out at the *Exposition* threw those doubts into even greater relief. The subject was once a living, breathing person, who had lived for a time in this very city. Marie-Angelique had walked the streets of Paris, as I had when we came to France, as well as the shores of Lake Michigan, as I had as a child. The more that was known about her, the less comfortable I felt about using that knowledge to "create" a character. What made it even more awkward was the fact that many people had written *about* Marie-Angelique, but there was nothing in the historical record in her own voice. In fact, that had become the very theme of my play – her struggle to escape being an object of observation, to be seen for who she was, and to speak her own truth. The more I learned about her, the more real she seemed and the more reluctant I became to take creative liberties with her story. The Wild Girl's very life had been mythologized, romanticized, and bent to the needs of others. The thought that I was a participant in that process made me very uneasy.

It wasn't so much a question of artistic freedom, which I believe in for myself and all artists. But context matters. As singular as her saga is, Marie-Angelique was also one of many millions of Indigenous people whose lives were irrevocably damaged by colonialism. Non-Indigenous writers – myself included – have approached her character as generically indigenous. But that changed with Aroles' findings, which do not prove but strongly suggest that Marie-Angelique came from a specific place and nation. I found myself growing more and more uncomfortable trying to speak in her voice. In truth, I was becoming more interested in the real person than the "character" I had created; in the true story rather than the fictional one. I still didn't know what to do about the play, but at the very least, I resolved to stop making stuff up about her. I wanted to seek out the truth of Marie-Angelique's life, freed from the needs, fantasies, and projections of others – including my own – and to rescue her from the feral-child fables and restore her to her real-life personhood.

The best-known part of Marie-Angelique's story is the time she lived as a wild child in the woods. Her contemporaries judged from her animal-like behaviors that her time in the wilderness was fairly lengthy. In his timeline of her life, Aroles came to the conclusion that it was an astounding ten years, which for a long time struck me as highly improbable – until I stumbled across the story of another woman who had survived an even longer period of "lost years" in the wilderness. There were parallels between the two that I found nothing short of remarkable. Like Marie-Angelique, the Lone Woman of San Nicolas Island was Indigenous, and her story had been similarly fictionalized and fable-ized. As was also the case with Marie-Angelique, the true story of what happened to the Lone Woman was far more compelling than the fairy tale.

CHAPTER 8
The Lone Woman

"In this deserted spot, for eighteen years, a human being lived alone. Here she was found at last by fishermen who are living, and whose affidavits, properly witnessed, stamp as true every detail of the remarkable incident."

- from *The Lone Woman of San Nicolas Island* by Emma Hardacre

As the author of several young adult novels (YA, as they're known in the trade), I can't help feeling a twinge of jealousy for Scott O'Dell. In the late 1950s, he was already a successful author when he submitted his latest manuscript to his editor at Houghton Mifflin. The editor said she liked it very much, but she thought the book was better aimed at child readers. O'Dell was surprised – he'd already published several novels and non-fiction books for adults and assumed this one would join them on bookstore shelves. He ultimately decided to trust his editor's judgement, which turned out to be a very wise decision. Published in 1960, *Island of the Blue Dolphins* received glowing reviews and went on to win the prestigious Newbery Medal for Children's Literature in 1961. To date the book has sold over eight million copies and is now considered a classic. The writer who never intended to write for kids went on to write two dozen more YA books and became one of the best-selling children's authors of all time. And, like JK Rowling, he hit the jackpot on his first try.

The title of O'Dell's book was familiar to me, though I didn't really know what it was about. I assumed it had something to do swimming with dolphins (which the heroine does at one point). I also knew the book had been made into a movie, which was vaguely confused in my mind with *The Blue Lagoon*, a film about two picture-perfect youth (one of them fourteen-year-old Brooke Shields), who fall in love while marooned on a tropical island. As it turned out, being marooned on an island was a common element of both stories. But it was only while working on this book that I became aware of the *Island of the Blue Dolphins* narrative, about a twelve-year-old girl named Karana who fends for herself for several years on an island off the California coast, after being left behind by rest of her tribe. Another story of a female surviving on her own in the wilderness? I had to get my hands on a copy.

Island of the Blue Dolphins opens with an idyllic scene of life in Karana's village. She and her younger brother Ramo are gathering spring roots when they spy an approaching ship; an unfamiliar sight on their remote island. The ship is bearing a band of Indigenous hunters from the Aleutian Islands, led by a Russian captain, who announces they have come to hunt sea otters. After a series of tense encounters over the next several days, a violent argument breaks out between the villagers and the hunters. When it's over, more than half the men in the village have been killed, including Karana's father. The Russian ship leaves but, vulnerable to other attacks due to their reduced numbers, Karana's people send an envoy in a dugout canoe for help. Rescuers arrive to evacuate what remains of the tribe, but as their ship pulls away from the island, Karana sees that her brother has been left behind. In a panic, she plunges into the sea and swims back to the island. The two of them wait for the ship to come back for them, but it doesn't. When Ramo goes off by himself in an attempt to prove his manhood, he gets attacked and mauled to death by a band of wild dogs. The scene of Karana discovering her brother's body and carrying his corpse back to the now-deserted village is almost unbearably sad. She is left all alone on the island, waiting and hoping that someone will return for her. For a revered children's book, *Island of the Blue Dolphins* is awfully rough going at the beginning.

O'Dell has rightly been praised for his feminist sympathies – the majority of his books feature strong female protagonists, the type of heroines often referred to as "plucky." But Karana is of another order of tough resourcefulness altogether. Her efforts to survive alone on the island become the focus of the story. During that time, she builds herself several shelters, catches fish to eat, rebuilds a damaged canoe, and makes weapons to hunt cormorants and elephant seals – in defiance of tribal tradition that only men are allowed to hunt and build weapons. She survives storms, an earthquake, and a tsunami. In a climactic scene, she emerges victorious in a battle with a giant octopus (called a devilfish in the book). But as time goes on and her isolation continues, the story takes an almost fairy-tale turn. She befriends an otter and tames two wild birds for pets. She tries to kill the leader of the wild dog pack to avenge her brother's death, and then nurses him back to health after which he becomes her trusted companion. A ship finally arrives to rescue her. As the book ends, she bids a bittersweet farewell to her island paradise, grateful that her lonely isolation has at last come to an end.

O'Dell intentionally left the amount of time Karana spends on the island vague, but references in the text to weather and seasonal markers indicate that it's at least four years. Here was another account of a person surviving in the wild over a long period of time, and I was curious to see how this section of the novel compared with Aroles' effort to document Marie-Angelique's "ten lost years" in the Champagne forest. There's a sense that both writers are trying to imagine the unimaginable; a human completely isolated from other humans, with no objective other than to stay alive another day. They also both have to grapple with the fact that the day-to-day details of survival – finding food to eat or a safe place to sleep – don't exactly make gripping reading. Aroles fills in the blanks of Marie-Angelique's sojourn with weather events and factual bits of contemporaneous history. O'Dell, on the other hand, seems undaunted by the possibility of boring readers. The middle section of *Island of the Blue Dolphins*, which constitutes the bulk of the text, reads like a how-to manual for surviving on a Pacific Island rather than a YA adventure. O'Dell has done copious research – not on what was happening in the wider world, as Aroles did, but on Indigenous cultures and methods of wilderness survival – and he is eager to share it all with his readers. The minutiae of detail O'Dell delves into – he gives a step-by-step account of how Karana fashions a spear out of a seal bone, for example – make some sense, given that he thought he was writing for adults. (From what I could glean from Internet sites like Goodreads, kid readers of *Island of the Blue Dolphins* are divided between those who are completely enthralled by the detail and those who are bored silly by it.) It's interesting to note that O'Dell also wrote a later novel, *Sarah Bishop*, about a girl who lived alone in the woods of New York State during the American Revolutionary War. She was known as the "Hermitess of West Mountain," and her story comes replete with animal friends and, like *Island of the Blue Dolphins* and much of O'Dell's fiction, is based on a historical fact.

An earlier book of O'Dell's, *Country of the Sun*, had briefly touched on the true-life story that inspired *Island of the Blue Dolphins*. A woman known to history as The Lone Woman of San Nicolas actually lived alone on this island off the coast of Santa Barbara, California for eighteen years in the mid-nineteenth century. Like Karana, she was left behind during an evacuation of the island, but it was her own child she went back to retrieve, not a brother. O'Dell made the character of Karana more than two decades younger than her real-life counterpart, who was judged to be in her mid-fifties when she was rescued from San Nicolas in 1853. In other ways he adhered quite closely to the facts in constructing his narrative. O'Dell benefitted from the availability of a source that was nearly contemporary with the events surrounding the Lone Woman of San Nicolas; an 1880 magazine article by historian Emma Hardacre. He also drew on the work of pioneering cultural anthropologist A. L. Kroeber, especially Kroeber's 1925 book *Handbook of the Indians of California.*

If anything, the parallels between the real-life story of the Lone Woman and Marie-Angelique's saga are even more striking than between the latter and O'Dell's novel. The two women's stories unfolded almost exactly a century apart; Marie-Angelique, born around 1712, emerged from the wild in 1731, while the Lone Woman of San Nicolas was likely born circa 1800, abandoned on the island in 1835 and brought back to civilization in 1853. They share a near-mythical status – the popular media of the day referred to the Lone Woman as "the Female Crusoe" – that came to overshadow the fact that they were actual persons living in a specific time and place. Both women's stories feature objects that have mysteriously gone missing; Marie-Angelique's cudgel, bearing markings that Burnett hoped would reveal her country of origin, and the Lone Woman's skirt made of satin-y green cormorant feathers, an object that made a deep impression on the search party who found her. After Juana Maria's death, her cormorant skirt was supposedly sent to the Vatican, never to be seen again. (Perhaps one day Serge Aroles will come across it during one of his forays into the Vatican Secret Archives.)

Both were baptized and given Christian names – when the woman was brought from San Nicolas to Santa Barbara, the mission priest there named her Juana Maria – but the birth names of both women are lost to history. Both of them became deathly ill soon after they were rescued – likely caused in both cases from a sudden change in diet from wild foods to cultivated ones. Marie-Angelique survived her ordeal, but Juana Maria died six weeks after her arrival in Santa Barbara. Both were visited by the curious and "studied" by experts of the time, particularly with a view to finding ways to overcome communication barriers. As we saw earlier, Marie-Angelique managed to learn (or more likely, re-learn) French. James Burnett believed that her first language was a variant of Huron-Wendat, while Serge Aroles' findings that she was Fox / Meskwaki seem to settle the question. (Fox / Meskwaki is part of the Algonquian family of languages.) Juana Maria did not live long enough to learn English or Spanish, and no one was ever found who could speak her language of origin, which remains a mystery to this day.

The most striking similarity, of course, is that both were Indigenous. Growing up in their respective Native communities would have given both women the wilderness knowledge and hunter-gatherer skills they later drew on to survive their solitary sojourns. Their Indigenous identities also exerted a powerful influence over how their stories of survival were viewed in the non-Native cultures into which they were introduced after being rescued. Some Santa Barbara residents did not believe that Juana Maria was an Indian because she seemed so gentle, modest, and un-savage. (One theory was that she was a European "lady of distinction," who was somehow cast away on San Nicolas by a shipwreck.)

We've already seen how Marie-Angelique's adult life in France was marked by the pain of being considered a freak, a curiosity, a "stranger in a strange land." Juana Maria never had to cross that cultural divide, since she lived only a few weeks after she was brought to Santa Barbara. But so much of her adult life had been spent apart from other humans, and she must have shared some of Marie-Angelique's profound sense of loneliness and alienation. As Hardacre put it, Juana Maria "drooped under civilization, she missed the outdoor life of her island camp." It's possible that it was the shock of her re-entry into human society – as much as her altered diet – that caused her death so soon after being rescued.

A Human Footprint

The Lone Woman's story of abandonment and rescue is every bit as astonishing as the saga of the Wild Girl of Champagne. Like Mme. Hecquet's and James Burnett's interviews with Marie-Angelique, Juana Maria had her own chronicler in the person of Emma Hardacre. Hardacre's article, published in *Scribner's Magazine* in 1880, conveyed Juana Maria's remarkable story to the world in a fact-based, journalistic format. A significant difference is that, unlike Hecquet and Burnett, Hardacre was never able to meet Juana Maria. But she did interview all the other principals within a couple of decades from when the events had taken place. Crucial among those was the chief rescuer, George Nidiver, the head of the expedition that searched for and ultimately found the Lone Woman. Of course, the accounts depend on the reliability and veracity of Hardacre's sources – it beggars belief, for example, that any of them could have gotten such a highly detailed account of her abandonment from Juana Maria herself, given that no one in Santa Barbara could understand her language.

For a long time before she was rescued, the Lone Woman of San Nicolas existed as a ghostly figure in the realm of local myth. For years stories circulated among the residents of Santa Barbara about a young woman who leapt from a ship to save her child and was accidentally left behind. There were occasional sightings of a solitary figure seen on the shore of the island from passing ships. One crew even went ashore and found the remains of a shelter made of whales' ribs planted in a circle. The structure was thought to have been the former residence of the chief of the tribe who had inhabited San Nicolas many years ago. Then, in the early 1850s, Nidiver brought a crew to the island to hunt and trap otters. While there, one of the crew thought he saw a human figure in the distance, but it quickly vanished. Nidiver led two more expeditions to San Nicholas, and in 1853, on their third trip to the island, he spied a human footprint in the sand. He decided to mount a thorough search of the dense inland area, and in subsequent days the crew found several more shelter-type structures, with baskets, fishing line, bone knives, rope and other objects indicating a human presence. Finally, they found more footprints and followed them up a cliff. One of the hunters encountered a woman and began to approach her. A pack of dogs growled at him, but she silenced them with a verbal command. When he spoke to her, she started to run away, then turned toward the hunter and began to address him in an unknown tongue. When the rest of the crew arrived, she greeted them and set about preparing a meal of roasted roots for them. Through her gestures, Nidiver said he was able to glean an account of how she'd survived all those years on the island: She showed them how she made fire by sparking sticks, to cook fish and shellfish. Through gestures, they communicated that she was to go with them. She understood immediately and put her things in pack baskets.

On arrival in Santa Barbara, people flocked to Nidiver's home to see her. Through gestures, she told Nidiver's wife that dogs had eaten her baby and how she grieved its loss. He reports that her speech was completely unintelligible to Chumash Indians in the area and to Indians from Santa Catalina Island as well. She got weaker and weaker and when she was near death, Nidiver's wife asked Father Sanchez to baptize her. He did so, giving her the name Juana Maria. She was buried in the walled cemetery beside the Santa Barbara Mission, but her grave site was left unmarked.

More recent research has expanded on Hardacre's first-hand accounts. Archaeological evidence indicates that San Nicolas, like the other Channel Islands, has been populated for at least 10,000 years, though perhaps not continuously. It is thought the Nicoleños (as the inhabitants of San Nicolas have come to be known) were closely related to the peoples of Santa Catalina and San Clemente Islands; Uto-Aztecan people related to the modern-day Tongva. The massacre of the Nicoleños has also been reliably documented. In 1811, a party of Aleuts and Russian fur traders landed on San Nicolas in search of sea otter and seal. They killed many of the Nicoleño men and raped many of the women, leaving the population decimated. By the 1830s only around a handful of Nicoleños remained. Reports of their dire situation reached the mainland, and a rescue mission arrived at the island in 1835. All but one of the tribe boarded the ship – the woman who would later be known as Juana Maria. Weather and other factors prevented further rescue attempts until the 1850s, when it was discovered, almost by accident, that she had survived.

The Canon of Sentiment

It's striking to note just how closely O'Dell adhered to the original account of the Lone Woman. But he didn't restrict himself to the details in Hardacre's 1880 article. He also drew on the work of pioneering cultural anthropologist A. L. Kroeber. In his 1925 book *Handbook of the Indians of California*, Kroeber describes many elements of the coastal peoples' lifestyle that appear in *Island of the Blue Dolphins:* Dwellings fashioned out of whale ribs, dugout canoes made from drift logs, a diet of seafood including abalone, scallops, mussels, and sea urchins, supplemented by with wild roots. (It's interesting to note that Kroeber was the father of the great Ursula K. LeGuin, a writer who also drew on anthropological sources for her fiction, but with much greater depth and knowledge than O'Dell.)

Like Serge Aroles with Marie-Angelique, O'Dell had little to go on to create Karana's story, and like Aroles, he drew on his abundant research to flesh out an entire life history for her. His task was complicated by the fact that the people who had inhabited San Nicolas died out in the nineteenth century. To fill in the gaps, he turned to the research of Kroeber and other anthropologists, freely inserting practices from other tribes into the Nicoleños' way of life. For example, in *Island of the Blue Dolphins* Karana bears a line of blue clay across her nose and cheekbones to indicate that she is unmarried. This is a variation on the face-painting practices of adolescent girls common among California tribes. And Karana's people have two names, a public one and a secret name, which must be carefully guarded to retain its power, a detail likely borrowed from Kroeber's account of the Yahi people.

Throughout his career O'Dell returned to Indigenous themes again and again, focussing especially on female protagonists including Sacagawea, Pocahontas, and Kapkap-Ponmi, the daughter of Nez Perce Chief Joseph. *Island of the Blue Dolphins* was O'Dell's first foray into Indigenous-themed fiction. When it was first published in 1980 it was praised for its sympathetic view of Native people and hailed as an antidote to the bloodthirsty, tomahawk-wielding Indians of Hollywood westerns.

Present-day Indigenous scholars have less patience with these well-meaning but inaccurate narratives. Debbie Reese, a Nambe Pueblo and specialist in children's literature, argues that readers' uncritical acceptance of stereotypical depictions of American

Indians is the real reason for the popularity of O'Dell's book. She says Karana's manner of speaking without using contractions, her use of phrases like "many moons ago" are time-worn, clichéd depictions of Indian speech, and finds O'Dell's and other white authors' generic approach to Indian life particularly annoying – "as though one peoples' way of being was interchangeable with another." Reese admits that judging O'Dell's half-century-old work by contemporary standards may seem a bit harsh, but she believes that good intentions aren't enough to justify the book's place in the kid-lit pantheon.

Reese also aims her critique at the nostalgic yearning for the romantic "Indian" of yesteryear – living in the pristine wilderness, where the air is pure and the water is clean. Closely related to this is the trope of the "Vanishing Indian" – noble, brave, and doomed to disappear from the face of the earth. (The phrase "the last of her tribe" appears again and again in accounts of the Lone Woman of San Nicolas.) *Island of the Blue Dolphins* is an example of what Reese calls the "canon of sentiment" – books and films that "give the audience the kind of Indians that America loves to love."

There is a nub of truth in that sentimental view. Many non-Natives harbor the belief that the Indian way of life really IS superior. That was certainly the conclusion reached by the white women featured in the next chapter, who, like Marie-Angelique, were forcibly removed from their families and had to adapt to a culture utterly unlike what they had known as children. But in the last analysis, what the canon of sentiment argues most forcefully for is for non-Natives to put aside our own fantasies and try viewing these stories through an Indigenous lens.

CHAPTER 9
Women Between Worlds

"She was dressed as an Indian, she lived as one, and at length she had well-nigh forgotten how to speak English. Three years passed and it was reported that she herself was unwilling to leave the life she had adopted."

-from *An Unredeemed Captive: Being the Story of Eunice Williams, who at the Age of Seven Years, was Carried Away from Deerfield by the Indians in the Year 1704, and who Lived Among the Indians in Canada as One of Them the Rest of Her Life* by Clifton Johnson, 1897

Ever since that September day in 1731, when the sight of her sent terrified villagers screaming, "The devil has come to Songy!", the Wild Girl has stirred up extreme reactions. The villagers' fear was quite understandable – this was a sight like nothing they had ever seen before; a creature entirely unknown in their previous experience. Though they soon discovered that "it" was human and female, they knew for certain that she was an Other, a Not-Us, and this profound sense of "otherness" marked her to the end of her days. It was through the process of becoming "civilized" that Marie-Angelique acquired the peculiarly Christian sentiments of shame and self-loathing. She could never escape who she was, how she was seen, and what people knew about her – that she had stripped naked and jumped into the moat, that she ate raw flesh, that she had killed a dog with a club. As Serge Aroles says, Marie-Angelique's was a life like no other, unparalleled and unique in human history. Her predicament aroused a range of responses – disgust, fascination, and even sympathy – in the people who encountered her, either firsthand or through the sensational accounts of eighteenth-century print media.

Those accounts should be viewed through the lens of what we know about eighteenth-century notions of "the Savage." There is a distinction to be made between the English word "savage" – variously defined as "fierce, violent, primitive, uncivilized" – and the French "*sauvage*," which has the more neutral primary meaning of "wild," or "in an untamed state of nature." (literally "of the forest," from the Latin *sylvaticus*). But it's really more a question of semantics rather than a substantive distinction, because the perceptions of a savage *person* were common to all European cultures. From their earliest contact with Indigenous people, Europeans didn't even consider them human, until a Papal Bull in 1537 decreed that they were human enough to try converting them to Christianity. In her groundbreaking book *The Myth of the Savage and the Beginnings of French Colonialism in the Americas,* Indigenous historian Olive Dickason traces the development of the concept from earliest contact through the rise and fall of New France. Europeans encountering Amerindians saw them as unreasoning beasts in a state of nature, coarse and indifferent to suffering. The Amerindians were mystified by the notion of land ownership and private property, and foolishly – in the eyes of Europeans – didn't try to acquire more than they needed. They appeared to lack any formal system of government – an impression that in time was completely overturned as historians learned of institutions like the Confederacy of the Six Iroquois Nations, now known as Haudenosaunee. To European ears, Indigenous languages sounded like pure gibberish – until they had to learn them in order to carry on trade, and discovered that they were highly sophisticated grammatical and aural constructions. The colonialists were wrong about almost everything they believed about Indians. But they knew for certain that these people were lesser beings than Europeans.

Colonial attitudes were also influenced by a folkloric figure that had had wide currency throughout Europe since medieval times. The Wild Man of the Woods (*Homo Sylvestris* in Latin) had much in common with the characteristics listed above, but his most outstanding feature was his pre-Christian, pagan nature. Which certainly fit with Europeans' view of their early encounters in the Americas – that the "backwardness" of Indigenous people was rooted in their paganism, their ignorance of the One True God. In fact, though, the project of colonial conquest was driven by unmistakably economic motives – all those trees and beaver pelts were worth big money in Europe – its stated aim was to convert the "savages" to Christianity and save their souls. Which is why Marie-Angelique's testament of faith had such resonance for Mme. Hecquet and her readers: "Would God deliver me from the wild beasts and make me Christian, only to abandon me afterwards, to let me die of hunger? No, that is impossible." This much-quoted statement served to reinforce belief in the fundamental rightness of the great Christian project, which was to convert the savage tribes of North American.

In her book, Dickason tells of a theatre play with a fictional "Indian" character that also likely influenced reaction to the Wild Girl. The play, *Arlequin Sauvage,* depicted a character who, like Marie-Angelique, was transplanted to Europe. It was produced in a Paris theatre in 1721, ten years before the Wild Girl emerged from the forest. In this case, the lead character was more of a bumbling innocent than the near-demonic figure of the pagan Wild Man of the Woods. But history shows time and again that the pagan beast and the noble savage are simply two sides of the same coin. Views of the savage were also influenced by the eighteenth-century wave of intellectual interest in the then-nascent concept of evolution. In *Systema Naturae*, his famous work of taxonomic classification, biologist Carl Linneaus assigned the Wild Girl to her own unique category: *Puella*

Campanica. In some of his later writings, Charles Burnett toyed with the idea that Marie-Angelique might be something akin to the fabled "Missing Link" between ape and human, between savagery and civilization. These ideas might have originated as honest intellectual investigations, but Europeans, especially those who emigrated to "the colonies," readily adopted them as racist tropes.

Stolen Sisters

Having embarked on a quest to de-mythicize Marie-Angelique's life, I was glad to finally encounter a YouTube video in an out-of-the-way corner of the Internet that clearly arose from an Indigenous perspective. "Marie-Angelique et Moi" by Canadian spoken-word poet Winona Linn, is a moving tribute that speaks from Linn's own Indigenous roots and packs a fierce denunciation of colonialism into its just-under-four-minute length. Particularly powerful is the way Linn refers to Marie-Angelique as one of many "stolen sisters," placing her in the larger historical context of thousands of Indigenous women whose existence has been wiped out in recent decades.

This is a growing issue on both sides of the North American border. In many cases the women are known to have been murdered, but in others they have simply gone missing, leaving behind grieving families who may never know what became of them. In 2016, the Canadian government established a National Inquiry into Missing and Murdered Indigenous Women and Girls, and two years later the U.S. declared May 5 a National Day of Awareness for Missing and Murdered Indigenous Women and Girls. The acronym MMIW has become well-known in both countries as a standalone reference, often rendered as MMIWG and MMIWG2S to include girls, and 2-Spirit People, respectively. Canadian statistics show without doubt that Indigenous women are frequent targets of hate, and it's estimated that they're nearly four times more likely to be victims of violent crime than non-Native women Many of these instances have occurred on the so-called "Highway of Tears," a 700-kilometre stretch of Highway 16 in British Columbia that has been the site of innumerable murders and disappearances of Indigenous women since the late sixties.

With so many unnknowables in the case of MMIW, the contrast between couldn't be more stark when the stolen women are white. Historically, the taking of settler hostages by Indigenous tribes occurred much less frequently, But incidents of it were abundantly documented in sensationalist accounts by nineteenth-century white writers. These mass-market books served as cautionary tales for other settlers, helping to create the image of marauding Indians defiling pure white women, similar to the myths about black men in the South. The most widely-known case is that of Cynthia Ann Parker, whose story formed the basis for the acclaimed American film *The Searchers*. In 1836, ten-year-old Cynthia Ann was abducted by a Comanche war party during a raid on her family's Texas settlement. She was adopted by the tribe and given the name Naduah, meaning "someone found." She lived with them for twenty-four years, completely forgetting her language and the ways of white society. She married a Comanche chieftain and had three children with him, including a son, Quanah, who would become famous as the last free Comanche chief.

Naduah's relatives never accepted her choice. When she was in her early thirties, after she'd lived as a Comanche for over two decades, a band of Texas Rangers raided her village. Identifying her by her blue eyes, they seized her and returned her to her white relatives. She escaped and more than once attempted to return to her Comanche husband and children but was re-captured and brought back to her family. She spent the next decade adamantly refusing to re-adjust to white society. Inconsolably heartbroken over the separation from her Comanche family, she starved herself to death in 1871.

Naduah's story captured the imagination of the entire nation, in news reports and later retellings. Wikipedia lists no fewer than a dozen fictional adaptations of her life, including the 1954 book by Alan Lemay, which was adapted for the film. In both book and film, Cynthia Ann's uncle, James W. Parker provided the model for the central character, Ethan Edwards (played by John Wayne), who spent years in an obsessive, unabashedly racist quest to return his niece to white society. In the film, Edwards' intention is to kill his niece, believing she's "better off dead" after contamination by living with Indians. *The Searchers* was a commercial and critical success and has come to be considered a masterpiece. It has a place on numerous "best of" lists, including twelfth on the American Film Institute's 100 greatest films ever made. But the enshrining of *The Searchers* in the film pantheon hasn't been without controversy. Some view *The Searchers* as a blatantly racist film, based on the character of Ethan Edwards and the portrayal of the Comanche as vicious, bloodthirsty savages, while some advocates for *The Searchers* argue that, in laying bare the racism of the John Wayne character, it's really an *anti*-racist film, using an all-American genre to question U.S. history and its heroes.

There's another case of an abducted white woman, who was born around the same time as Marie-Angelique and, like the Wild Girl, was taken from her family and lived out her life between two profoundly different worlds. Unlike Marie-Angelique, she never lost the knowledge of who she was and where she came from. Despite given multiple opportunities to return to her original home and family, she chose not to.

Eunice Williams was born in Deerfield, Massachusetts, on September 17, 1696, the daughter of a prominent Puritan minister and his wife. Eunice had a conventional and privileged New England childhood, which ended with sudden violence when she was seven years old. In the pre-dawn hours of February 29, 1704, a force of about 300 French and Native allies launched a daring raid on the English settlement of Deerfield, Massachusetts, an event that became known as the Deerfield Massacre. Eunice's family home was attacked and two of her younger siblings were killed, including her baby sister. Eunice, her parents, and her other four siblings were taken captive and forced to march hundreds of miles north through cold and deep snow. On the second day of the march their captors decided that Eunice's mother, having recently given birth, was too weak to travel, and slaughtered her.

Bloodthirsty Indians, helpless female captives – it reads like a pulpy Hollywood Western. In fact, the raid on the town of Deerfield was one of many in the conflict known as Queen Anne's War, the second in a series of wars fought between Great Britain and France for control of the North American continent. During the conflict, English settlements in New England were subject to brutal raids by French forces and their Native allies. Like Marie-Angelique, Eunice Williams was a child of war.

Eunice was separated from the rest of her family and taken to the village of Kahnawake, which at that time was also the site of a Catholic mission overseen by Jesuit priests. She was adopted into a Mohawk family, and — to the horror of her Puritan kin — converted to Catholicism. She took Marguerite as a baptismal name, and was also given a Mohawk name; Waongote, which roughly means "planted as a member of the tribe." As she grew up she became fully assimilated into Kahnawake life, taking on the duties of a Mohawk woman; planting and harvesting the three main crops of corn, squash, and beans, as well as collecting firewood, preparing food, and making clothing. In 1713 she married a Mohawk man, Arosen, who had also converted to Catholicism, taking François Xavier as his baptismal name. With him she bore several children, only two of whom survived to adulthood. At a later point in life, following tribal custom, she acquired yet another name appropriate to her age and status; Gannenstenhawi, meaning "she brings in corn."

Back in New England, her relatives mourned her loss and worked relentlessly for her return. But it soon became clear that Eunice herself had no interest in being rescued. Her father, having been freed and returned to Deerfield, traveled to Canada to see her, but was flatly rebuffed. Other emissaries, acting on his behalf, fared no better. Marguerite made clear to them that she wished to remain in her Mohawk community. In the last few decades of her life, Marguerite Gannenstenhawi did travel to her original home in the Connecticut Valley on four separate occasions, accompanied by her husband. Each time, her Williams relatives hoped and prayed that she would decide to stay for good. But these were visits, nothing more. For the rest of her long life she remained firmly — and, from the Christian standpoint, tragically — an "unredeemed captive," echoing the title of historian John Demos' authoritative account of her life.

The seed of her choice might be found in her experience of the long march. When the child Eunice stumbled and fell from exhaustion, she was taken under the wing of one of her captors, an Indian man who carried her on his shoulders through mile after mile of deep snow. At night he covered the child with a blanket. This unnamed Mohawk became Eunice's protector on the long march to Canada and was likely related to the family into which she was adopted in Kahnawake.

Still, it strains belief that she would form bonds with the very people who kidnapped her family and killed her mother. In the English colonies, she became a stark symbol of the danger that "civilized" (i.e., white) people might somehow be turned into "savages." They were convinced that she had undergone a kind of brainwashing, a victim of what is known in modern times as the Stockholm Syndrome, in which kidnapping victims develop a psychological alliance with their captors as a survival strategy. (Think of the images from the seventies of heiress Patti Hearst, wielding a machine gun in bank heists beside her kidnappers, the Symbionese Liberation Army.) But it's worth noting that, among the Deerfield captives, Eunice was far from the only one who chose to stay. Many of the younger captives, mostly children and teenagers at the time of the raid, also opted to remain permanently with adoptive Indian families. This was true for girls in particular; there were nine who stayed as opposed to five boys. In fact, overall among colonial captives, a higher proportion of females chose to remain in Native society rather than return to colonial settlements. We can only speculate about the reasons for this, but the high status of women in Indian societies – female elders in particular – could well have been a factor.

Most of what we know about Eunice comes from the writings of her father, John Williams, who wrote *The Redeemed Captive Returning to Zion*, about his experience. Published in 1707, the book framed the raid and captivity, and border relations with the French and Indians in terms of Divine Providence. Williams' account stood out among the many captivity narratives of the time, especially in the way he transformed the genre into a celebration of his own heroism in holding to Protestant values in the face of attacks from "savages" and Catholics alike. *The Redeemed Captive* was widely read in the New England colonies, and is a major reason why the Deerfield raid is still remembered and well known today.

Reverend John Williams died in 1729, still estranged from his daughter. But some time in the years after his death, Marguerite Gannenstenhawi had a change of heart. In August of 1740, Stephen and Eleazer Williams traveled to Albany for what Stephen described as a "joyful, sorrowful meeting of our poor sister that we had been separated from for above 36 years." Arosen and Gannenstenhawi accompanied her brothers back to Stephen's home in Longmeadow, Massachusetts, and stayed there for about a week. Arosen and Gannenstenhawi left with promises that, now that the way was open, they would return for a longer visit, and they did, on three occasions. Marguerite Gannenstenhawi's final visit to New England came in 1761, when she was sixty-four. As in previous visits, the Williams family gathered at Longmeadow from various points in Massachusetts and Connecticut, and neighbors flocked to the church to see the returned captive. Stephen never gave up on his attempts to convince his sister to stay in Massachusetts, but he was unsuccessful. From time to time in the years after the last visit, he heard news about her, including that her husband, Arosen, died in 1765. Surviving records from Kahnawake show the births and baptisms of their two daughters, who lived with their mother well into her old age. Marguerite Gannenstenhawi, formerly known as Eunice Williams, died at Kahnawake in November 1785 at the age of 89.

Gannenstenhawi was no means unique. In Colonial times, captive-taking by Native Americans was not uncommon. Some were killed, some became war hostages but many, especially children, were taken for the purpose of adoption to replace lost family members, a custom which is difficult for the modern, non-Indigenous mind to comprehend. This is not to minimize the trauma of war, which always causes children the most suffering. Like Marie-Angelique, these children witnessed horrific brutality and suffered violent separation from their families and communities. But they were given the opportunity to return home, though many decided instead to stay with their Native families. These decisions to stay puzzled the Europeans to no end. They had come to America believing that converting the Natives would be easy, once they saw the superiority of European religion, language, clothing, and farming practices. Yet very few Natives adopted English culture – the overall trend went decidedly in the opposite direction. Benjamin Franklin was one of the few settler leaders to even consider that the captives might have a point, and to acknowledge their agency in their choice. He wrote of white children captured by Native tribes, that many "become disgusted with our manner of life and take the first good opportunity of escaping again into the woods, from whence there is no reclaiming them."

It was certainly not for lack of trying. The effort to reclaim stolen children is a perennial theme of captivity narratives dating back to the early days of contact between settlers and Indigenous people. The desire to reunite with loved ones and restore the bonds of family were equally strong among Natives and Europeans. One significant difference, however, was the added religious obligation borne by colonists to "redeem" stolen family members for Christianity, to rescue them from paganism and savagery, which many considered a fate worse than death.

At bottom, these stories about abducted white females who "cross over" to the Indigenous world are focussed mainly on the rescue narrative, in which the male protagonist must take back "his" women in order to reclaim his manhood. But there's another quality, a singular mystery that binds these stories. None of these women are ever able to speak in their own voices, to recount in their own words the experience of living in two worlds. Like Marie-Angelique, they were observed and written about by others. All we know about Eunice Williams comes to us through her father's account. Likewise with Cynthia Parker, we have only sensational news reports of the times, as well as numerous fictionalizations. There is nothing that tells us how the women felt, and why they made the choices they did.

Going Home Again

Emigration, the leaving of one place country to settle in another, has been part of the human experience for millennia. People choose to emigrate for a variety of reasons – to find better economic opportunities, to live in a more hospitable climate, to seek religious freedom. But just as often, the decision to emigrate is made with reluctance. In the case of refugees fleeing war or environmental disaster, in fact, it's a matter of sheer survival, barely a choice at all. The prospect of emigration carries far more emotional freight than a simple change of location: It means leaving one's culture, one's community, one's extended family, the place where one has a deep sense of belonging. It's something I feel connected to through my own ancestors, who fled Ireland during the Great Famine in the 1840s. The Irish, who lost a quarter of their population to death and emigration as a result of the famine, have a deep tradition of emigration ballads about the sorrow of leaving home and the unceasing longing to return.

Toronto, where I live, is widely regarded as the most multicultural city in the world. People from all over the globe come here to live, but we all know who we are and where we were born. We know who our parents and relatives are, and through them we're familiar with the cultural context that shaped us. The exception is adoptees, but even that is changing with the growing movement toward open adoption. Nowadays it's common for adoptees to search for their birth families and their right to the opening of previously-secret adoption records is widely acknowledged. In the modern world, being cut off from your roots is considered nothing short of a tragedy.

Here we arrive at yet another way Marie-Angelique Memmie LeBlanc was exceptional. Her life was lived out in two different places – her Indigenous North American homeland, and the European continent to which she was taken. But unlike the rest of us, she retained almost no memory of her past. What few fragments she did have served mainly as clues for the detective work of the Europeans who were trying to ascertain where she'd come from. We can only speculate about the effect this vacuum of memory had on her. How did she really feel when grilled by Hecquet or Burnett about dimly-recalled, inescapably painful events? One thing that is certain is that she was robbed of the opportunity to learn about where she came from, and to return there if she so chose. You can't go home again, if you don't know where home is.

I often wonder what Marie-Angelique would have done if she'd been able to discover her true origins. Would she have chosen to return her people? Like both Gannenstenhawi and Naduah, she became fully assimilated into the culture she was stolen away to. She read and spoke French, lived the urban life of an eighteenth-century *Parisienne,* even – according to Aroles - becoming wealthy in her later years. But unlike Gannenstenhawi and Naduah, whose choices were shaped by the fact that they had formed bonds with spouses, family, and community, Marie-Angelique's life appears to have been a solitary one. She lived in a series of convents, and later moved many times during her life in Paris. One of the main themes of my play was her experience of being a stranger in a strange land. At one point in my script, the character says that learning where she came from would serve no purpose. "If I were to return, the people there would say, 'Who are you? We do not know you. You are not one of us.' And they would be right. There is no place I belong in this world. I am a stranger to everyone, even to myself."

I was beginning to wonder about that. It was all well and good to write a passage of such lovely melancholy. But now I was more focussed on discovering the "real" Marie-Angelique, and I had to ask myself – how did I know that? Was it even true? Here was a woman whose life straddled the Indigenous and European worlds, yet almost all the existing accounts are Euro-centric and begin when she emerges from the Champagne forest. As far as I could determine, neither Aroles nor anyone else had contacted the Meskwaki nation about the Wild Girl. In fact, it appeared that hardly anyone from the Indigenous world even knew about her. Who were the

Meskwaki in the contemporary world? Did they know about the Wild Girl's history? Did they claim her as one of their own? Would they have said, "You are not one of us?" Or would they have welcomed her back?

I decided I'd have to ask them myself.

CHAPTER 10
The Red Earth People

"Know ye, that the Foxes are immortal."

-Pemoussa, Fox (Meskwaki) chief, 1712

Though the 2017 *Exposition* in Chalons-en-Champagne included Aroles' speculations on Marie-Angelique's early life, the overwhelming focus was on her time in France, where she'd spent most of her life. Talking to Isabelle Guyot, the librarian who had originally conceived the project, I found we shared the same concern. Impressive as the *Exposition* was, there was a big piece missing. The Wild Girl's story was incomplete, and we both wondered if there was a way to bring it full circle. Isabelle showed me a brochure she'd obtained in the course of her research, from a group called the *Communauté Mesquakie du Canada*, bearing a logo of a red circle with the words "Renards Nation." The brochure described a number of weekend courses in such subjects as forest survival, medicinal herbs, edible wild plants, even tanning animal hides. We were both fascinated. Here were people of Fox ancestry, teaching traditional Indigenous ways in a modern context. The brochure bore an address in St. Paulin, a town in the Mauricie region of Quebec, a ninety-minute drive north of Montreal. I told Isabelle that I would look into the group when I got back to Canada.

I still had some reservations about how completely the *Exposition* and the BD had embraced Aroles' view that Marie-Angelique was Meskwaki. It would have been the mother of all ironies, of course, had Aroles' work turned out to be the kind of elaborate hoax that he'd exposed about other feral children. But no source I'd encountered in my own research suggested that was the case. I certainly didn't think it was. Even given his own reluctance to share his work with scholars and the public, there was an overall consensus about the plausibility of Aroles' findings. Apart from his work, all we know about the Wild Girl comes from sources nearly three centuries old. It would be awfully difficult for a contemporary researcher to uncover any more than Aroles had during his ten years in various archives. Absolute proof was not, and likely never would be, on the table. All history is a kind of storytelling about the past, after all. Often there is solid evidence of what happened, but sometimes we have to just make do with what we have.

When I did a web search of the group on the flyer Isabelle showed me, references to a book kept popping up. *Les Mesquakie du Canada* is about some contemporary residents of Quebec who traced their ancestry back to the intermarriage of Fox slaves and French settlers in the eighteenth century. The author, Rejean Chauvette, has traced his own lineage seven generations back to a *Renard* ancestor. Chauvette is also the head of the *Communauté Mesquakie du Canada,* and the group even had a Facebook page. This was going to be a piece of cake! Or so I thought. As I searched the group further, I learned they regarded themselves as a newly-minted Métis "nation" and were part of a coalition of Quebec Métis groups, *l'Assemblée des Communautés Métisses Historiques du Québec.*

Now is a good time to pause and consider the knotty complexities of the term "Métis," from the French *metissé*, meaning "mixed." At its most literal, the term refers to people of mixed Indigenous and European heritage, but it also has a more specific meaning. When people in Canada use the term, they are usually referring to a specific group, the Métis Nation that historically resides in the Prairie provinces, chiefly Manitoba. Members of the Métis Nation have a culture, an ancestral language (Michif, a blend of Plains Cree and French), a common history and political traditions, and are connected through a vast kinship network. There are some who argue that this use of the term is too limited, that it excludes others in Canada who can legitimately claim mixed Indigenous-European identity. The question of who is Métis is a contentious one, especially in the province of Quebec.

Ancestry has long been a serious matter in French Canada. Inhabitants of Quebec have a phrase, *"pure laine,"* used to describe those whose ancestry is exclusively French-Canadian. Literally meaning *pure wool,* the term likely harks back to the 1700s, when raising sheep for wool was common. A term with a similar meaning is *"de souche,"* meaning stock or base of a tree. This preoccupation with French identity fits with a reluctance among Quebeckers to acknowledge the reality of French-Indigenous mixing in the province's history. In its extreme form, many were invested in having lineage from *Les Filles du Roi,* the myth that all present-day *Quebecois* are descended from 800 women sent to New France by King Louis XIV in the late-seventeenth century to provide wives for male colonists. The ostensible purpose was to increase the population of New France, but the obvious corollary was to reduce the incidence of intermarriage with Indigenous women, a practice widespread among the early traders known as *coureurs de bois.* We know now that intermarriage between Europeans and Indigenous people left a large legacy on the people and history of Quebec. Some modern researchers estimate that at least half and possibly three-quarters of all Quebecers have at least one aboriginal ancestor.

But the tide is turning. Claiming Indigenous roots is becoming almost chic in some quarters, and lately there's been a veritable flood of Quebec residents joining organizations allowing them to claim Métis status. A factor driving the newfound interest in Métis heritage is a 2016 Supreme Court decision, Daniels v. Canada, that ruled that the country's 600,000 non-status Indians and Métis people are considered Indians under the Constitution. Some groups allow anyone who can demonstrate any degree of aboriginal ancestry—through DNA or simply by showing genealogical documents—can apply for a "status" card, which costs $80 and promises its holder a series of entitlements such as free medication, which are available to status Indians.

Driven in part by the popularity of online genealogical and DNA testing sites like Ancestry and 23andMe, this reliance on self-identification poses some obvious problems. From the point of view of existing Indigenous communities, these Métis-come-latelies are motivated by the perceived perks of being Aboriginal. And the perks are considerable. With a status card you can buy a car and avoid the tax, saving up to $5,000 on a $35,000 purchase. Indian-rights activists are fiercely critical, arguing that it takes more than family stories or a long-lost ancestor for a person to claim citizenship in an Indigenous nation. Writer Chelsea Vowel says that such claims feed a "white fantasy of becoming 'Indian,'" and in fact work *against* the interests of Indigenous communities. Others agree that the growing number of individuals self-identifying as Métis pose a threat to hard-won rights for the historic Métis Nation and other Indigenous groups. One applicant found a Huron-Wendat ancestor on his mother's side and a Nipissing ancestor on his father's side, both from the 1600s. Based on this rationale, millions could claim Métis status, since almost every white *Québecois* has a tiny bit of Indigenous ancestry.

And the dilemma is not confined to Quebec. The complexities of blood quantum are having a political impact elsewhere in Canada and in the U.S. In New Mexico, there's an ongoing controversy concerning mixed-blood descendants of Natives and Hispanics who are claiming the right to call themselves Indians instead of Latinos, stimulating a broader debate over how Native Americans are identified, involving contentious factors like tribal membership.

The number of Canadians self-identifying as Métis has surged in the last decade, with many individuals who had previously identified as white now pointing to genealogical research to back up their claims of Indigeneity. So, I wondered whether the *Communauté Mesquakie du Canada* were yet another group of wannabe Indians. The more I looked into the issue, the more I was sure that I didn't want to wade into this quagmire. That may have been just as well, because my attempts to contact the group kept coming up empty. Their Facebook page hadn't been updated in two years, and most of the postings had to do with selling Native crafts. Elsewhere on the web I encountered vanishing message boards, Wordpress sites, and – by now I shouldn't be surprised – yet another book that can't be found. There were no copies of *Les Mesquakie du Canada* available on Amazon or any other bookselling sites. The National Library of Canada did list one copy, but said it was in the "off-site stacks" which didn't sound promising. Once again, I had to accept that my search had come to a dead end.

Having left North America when she was a child, Marie-Angelique left no descendants, and it was becoming all too clear that my hope of finding some link to her ancestors was a pipe dream. There was undoubtedly some Mesquakie DNA floating around Quebec, but as a group they had no real presence there. Claude Aubin of the *Nation Métis de Quebec* says that true First Nations people "already know who they are without doing genealogical research." He might have been talking about the present-day Meskwaki Nation, a group of people who know exactly who they are, and where they came from.

A Settlement, not a Reservation
When I first learned of Serge Aroles' belief that the child who would become Marie-Angelique was a Meskwaki who had been enslaved in the early-eighteenth century, I was a bit nonplussed. I thought I knew my Canadian history, but I had never heard of the Meskwaki Nation, much less the Fox Wars. I assumed the Meskwaki were a distant relic of the New France era. As the object of my ten-year search continued to prove elusive, I thought that learning about Marie-Angelique's people might help me give her more of a personal dimension. I had no idea how true that would turn out to be: The child who survived the trauma of war, abduction, and ten

years of wilderness solitude came from truly exceptional people, the Meskwaki – the most remarkable Indian Nation you've never heard of.

The Meskwaki are of Algonquian origin from the regions of the Eastern Woodland Culture. They trace their origins to the Lac St. Jean region in the St. Lawrence River Valley, but they have lived at various times in the present-day states of Massachusetts, Rhode Island, Michigan, Wisconsin, Illinois, Missouri, and Iowa. They've been known by almost as many names as the places they've lived. The French called them *les Renards,* the Fox people, because in the era of New France the tribe lived on the Fox River and controlled trade there. Some tribes in the Great Lakes region referred to them as the *Outagami* ("people of the other shore"), but Meskwaki, which means the "Red Earth People" is how they refer to themselves. (The alternate spelling, "Mesquakie" is still in use in Quebec and other places, but the nation officially adopted the spelling in the 1980s.) The Meskwaki spoken language is a dialect similar to those of other midwestern nations, such as the Kickapoo. The Meskwaki and Sauk (also known as Sac), though two distinct groups, have linguistic and cultural similarities and a longstanding historical relationship that continues into the present. (The Sauk have their own storied history, much of it revolving around Black Hawk, famed leader of the 1832 war to reclaim the tribe's territory from the U.S. government.)

The story of the Meskwaki Nation is similar to the many Indigenous peoples who were countless times forced to relocate by governments in both the United States and Canada. Despite some differences – e.g. the fact that what's known as a "reservation" in the U.S. is called a "reserve" in Canada – the present-day arrangements that govern most tribes are generally similar in the two countries. For the most part, Indigenous communities live under certain regulations, on land owned by the government, from which they derive certain benefits in exchange. But please don't call the Meskwaki settlement a "reservation," because in contrast to the majority of Indigenous nations, they own the land they live on.

That's far from the only thing that makes the Meskwaki distinctive. They lived their traditional lifestyle until well into the twentieth century, with many families continuing to live in oval huts known as *wickiups*. They were the subject of a famous, ground-breaking study from 1948 to 1960 led by anthropologist Sol Tax of the University of Chicago. The tribe began to explore entrepreneurial avenues to maintain their independence, and in 1987 they mounted a modest Bingo enterprise in the tribal gymnasium, which members hoped would bring in revenue for better housing, education, and social services. Controversy over the Bingo operation ushered in a strife-ridden period and a tribal governance crisis. As with many Indigenous communities across North America, there were fears that gambling posed a threat to traditional values and culture. Nevertheless, in late 1992 the tribe decided to expand into Class III gaming and opened the Meskwaki Bingo Casino Hotel complex. The move brought a higher standard of living to the settlement, with new cars and TV satellite dishes, and today the Meskwaki are among the more prosperous groups of Native Americans in the U.S.

But in no way have the Meskwaki offloaded their heritage in the process. For generations the settlement was viewed by white society as insular, a "cultural island" and criticized as primitive and "slow to modernize." But it was their fierce resistance to European encroachment and their ability to be selective in the customs they adopted from the outside world that ensured the survival of their traditional culture, especially with regard to religion, ceremony, and language. The community still has a high proportion of people who speak Meskwaki as their first language. About one-third of the residents speak it exclusively, with the rest being bilingual. The Meskwaki have a rich artistic culture, with a strong tradition of weaving and beadwork, and their artists create works in both traditional and contemporary styles. As far back as the seventeenth- century they were known for their resistance to Christian missionaries. While some Meskwaki adopted Christianity, to this day most still belong to medicine societies and practice their ancestral faith.

Perhaps the most decisive way the Meskwaki resisted assimilation was their refusal to send their children to government-run boarding schools. Around the turn of the century, the federal government set up schools across the country to educate and assimilate Native American children and youths according to Euro-American standards. Called Residential Schools in Canada, these boarding schools were creating for the express purpose of removing children from the influence of their Native heritage and assimilating them into the dominant culture. In Canada, children were very often forcibly removed from their families and communities. But when the U.S. government built a boarding school for the tribe in nearby Toledo, Iowa, the Meskwaki simply refused to send their children there. After a year there were only four students enrolled, and a couple of years later the school closed down entirely. The damage done by Residential Schools is still reverberating in Canadian society, a multi-generational trauma that the Meskwaki, with their unshakeable sense of their own identity, managed to avoid.

Today about 1,300 Meskwaki live on "the Sett," which has grown to nearly 8,000 acres. They continue to adhere to their own customs and traditions even as they actively participate in mainstream American life. Meskwaki language and culture are central to the elementary curriculum at the settlement school. The Nation also operates a tribal court, public works department, and police force. In terms of economic development, they maintain a foot in both worlds, creating and growing a number of Native-owned businesses marketing products like vape juice and their own brand of "Renards" cigarettes to the world beyond the settlement.

The main thread that runs through Meskwaki history is their tremendous determination to preserve the integrity of their culture in the face of adversity. Their efforts to retain their identity, language, religious beliefs, and social organization have, for the most part, been highly successful. Change has come, but more slowly than among most other tribes, with the result that many traditional Meskwaki have been able to adjust to the increasing demands, challenges, and opportunities of modern life without abandoning their

Native heritage. Like the Jews, the Meskwaki held on to their separateness through their years of wandering. Like so many other Native American tribes, the Meskwaki survived wars, epidemics, organized removals, attempted genocide, and theft of their ancestral lands. But they never lost sight of who they were. A particular quality of perseverance, a core of inner strength, seems to have permeated the Fox psyche from their earliest days right up to the present. Even the French grudgingly admitted that the Meskwaki were the most formidable adversaries they had ever faced. The Fox may not be quite immortal but it's not hard to see why they might think so – especially given the fact that the King of France had once vowed to wipe them off the face of the earth.

A Genocidal War

The more I learned about the Meskwaki people, the more I was struck by how Marie-Angelique's remarkable saga of survival was reflected in the history of the Nation that gave birth to her. Having lived through the first Fox War, the plague in Marseilles, and ten years in the wilderness, the odds were overwhelmingly against this woman, who nevertheless lived well into her seventies. The odds were similarly against the Meskwaki Nation. Like the child Marie-Angelique, they shouldn't have survived, but they did.

Ironically, in the years leading up to the first Fox War the Meskwaki took part in an historic treaty that could have assured the survival of their people for generations to come. In 1701, Augustin Legardeur de Courtemanche, an emissary from the governor general of New France, set out for Montreal from what is present-day Wisconsin, accompanied by a flotilla of canoes paddled by more than a thousand representatives of Great Lakes tribes. (If that name sounds familiar, it should: de Courtemanche's wife, Marie-Charlotte, was the owner of the young slave who would become the Wild Girl.) There they joined other tribes to mark the signing of a treaty known as The Great Peace of Montreal, an event that ended nearly a century of conflict for control of the fur trade between New France, the Haudenosaunee (Iroquois) Confederacy, and the Fox,

Huron-Wendat, Anishnaabe, and other Great Lakes Nations. This historic peace initiative held out hope that an Indigenous / European alliance based on mutual respect, dialogue, and negotiation was a real possibility.

Not that agreement among the parties – which included thirty-nine Indigenous nations – came easily. The negotiations went on for many weeks and ended with ceremonies lasting several days. (The original copy of the Great Peace of Montreal is kept in Library and Archives Canada, where the Meskwaki symbol of a fox can be seen at the bottom of the document along with other pictographic signatures.) Though most of the signees also pledged fealty to the King of France, the Meskwaki representative, Miskousouath, declined to do so, and instead gave a speech emphasizing the independence and sovereignty of his people. De Courtemanche and the other French officials were not surprised by this recalcitrance – time and again they'd found the Fox the most vexing of their Native allies.

Miskousouath's defiance turned out to be a sign of things to come. Hostilities between the French and the Fox continually surfaced in the next few years and relations broke down completely with the Siege of Detroit in 1712. This is the period that best fits Aroles' timeline of Marie-Angelique's life, during which he concludes that she was enslaved. What is clear is that many Fox men, women, and children were captured and enslaved between 1712-1716, and that peace efforts were scuttled by the refusal of the French to make good on a commitment to return them. Despite a clear directive from the French court, many colonists not only retained but continued to acquire new Fox slaves, using the justification that they were baptizing their slaves and saving their souls. Within Indigenous cultures, the return of captured enemies was one of the most important signifiers of a real truce. On this point the French broke their word and that, to the Meskwaki, was the ultimate betrayal.

Things deteriorated further in the years leading up to the second, much more destructive, Fox War. In 1728 King Louis XV issued a decree that ordered the complete extermination of the Meskwaki Nation, and with the help of their other Native allies, the French nearly succeeded. The long-term effect of the Fox Wars was that the Meskwaki were driven from their homeland in Fox River country, and their numbers were severely diminished. The Fox population went from over 6,500 in the early eighteenth century to a few hundred at the end of hostilities in the mid-1730s. It's no exaggeration to say that, for the Meskwaki, the Fox Wars resulted in a near-genocide. No wonder that the Meskwaki continue to nurse a 300-year old grudge against the French nation right up to the present day.

In the ensuing decades, the Meskwaki survivors fled south to the present-day states of Iowa and Illinois. These lands were hardly unfamiliar territory to them. For generations they'd ranged over their hunting and fishing grounds in what we now call the Midwest. Illinois and north-eastern Iowa served as the chief sanctuary for the survivors of the Fox Wars. They established villages on both sides of the Mississippi and the population gradually recovered. But their troubles at the hands of European settlers were far from over. In the late eighteenth century a new colonial power emerged from the American Revolutionary War. Having achieved independence from their British masters, the newly-formed United States of America had no intention of keeping within the confines of the Thirteen Colonies and embarked on an expansionary path to annex the rest of the continent. By the 1840s, its land-devouring maw had reached the Mississippi.

CHAPTER 11
The Last Tribe of Iowa

"The confederated tribes of Sacs and Foxes cede to the United States, forever, all the lands west of the Mississippi to which they have any claim or title, or in which they have any interest whatever."

- Article 1, Treaty of 1842

Having accomplished the near-annihilation of the Meskwaki Nation during the Fox Wars, midway through the eighteenth century, the French were revelling in their power and might, confident that their presence in North America would last forever. But pride goeth before a fall, as the saying goes, and that pretty much sums up the fate of the French in North America. Within a couple of decades of ending the Fox Wars, they were defeated by the British in the French and Indian War and were forced to surrender most of their New-World territories. The Royal Proclamation issued by George III in 1763 sealed the demise of French power in North America. In the end, it was New France, not the Meskwaki Nation, that was wiped off the map forever.

The Royal Proclamation is sometimes referred to as the "Indian Magna Carta." Many Indigenous scholars and activists point to it as the legal foundation of their land rights in North America. When I first heard this, I thought it very strange. Why would Native people regard a British document with the word "royal" in its title as having any validity whatsoever? They were already here – it was Europeans who stole their land! And what possible relevance could a nearly 300-year-old document have in the modern world? Colonialism was a great wrong, but it's ancient history, water under the bridge. That attitude is shared by the vast majority of those of us descended from Europeans settlers, but it's ignorant and uninformed. The process by which land in the Americas passed into non-Indigenous ownership was far more layered and complex. Not to suggest that the result of colonial aggression was anything but the wholesale theft of Indigenous land, but it didn't happen all at once. In fact, for the first couple of centuries, European governments and Indigenous nations largely dealt with one another as sovereign entities. The Europeans were fully aware that they were on land that wasn't theirs. Their tactics were bellicose, and their original purpose in invading the Americas was nakedly opportunistic. They wanted to acquire and exploit the continent's riches – the Spaniards' lust for Aztec gold, the French greed for animal furs, the insatiable British appetite for shipbuilding timber. To achieve these goals, Europeans knew they had no choice but to rely on Native people's superior knowledge of the land and its resources. They respected Indigenous knowledge, and they engaged in trade with Indigenous nations. Racist attitudes were in play, but initially the clash of cultures was a two-way street. Native people were disgusted by the smell of the seldom-washed Europeans, and found their religious beliefs bizarre, ridiculous. They were just as convinced of the superiority of their own cultures as Europeans were of theirs. For much of the early post-contact period, dealings between Natives and Europeans were on a relatively equal, nation-to-nation footing.

That relationship was at the heart of the Royal Proclamation. It was mostly a statement of Britain's victory over the French, a division of the spoils of war. But it also contained an inherent recognition of Indigenous sovereignty over North American land. The

RP even gave *back* some stolen Native lands, however temporarily. Most significantly, it created a jurisdictional boundary (known as the Proclamation line) between the British colonies on the Atlantic coast and American Indian lands (called the Indian Reserve) west of the Appalachian Mountains. For a brief period, it appeared that Europeans and Natives might co-exist peaceably on the North American continent, with each side keeping to its side of the line. But in a few short years, British settlements were encroaching on the land west of the Appalachians, and the exploitive practice of acquiring land via "negotiated" treaties was in full swing.

Subsequent to the War of Independence in 1776, the United States adopted the treaty approach to legitimize their territorial expansion in North America. The terms of these treaties were usually highly disadvantageous to the Native people, who often did not appreciate the implications of what they were agreeing to. The Indigenous concept of land ownership was and still is profoundly different from that of Europeans. It is a fluid and collectivist notion, revolving around land use and stewardship. In Native cultures, when a group of people were working a piece of land for agriculture, or seasonally occupying it for hunting grounds, that was considered a form of ownership. It's a notion closer to what the English call "the commons" – in which land is owned not by individuals but by the community as a whole. Of course, through history Indigenous nations have had plenty of disputes among themselves over particular parcels of land – disputes that often led to war. What they did not have was written deeds; certificates of permanent ownership, formalized by an exchange of goods or money.

When we look at modern maps, our attention turns immediately to the lines – mostly straight ones – that delineate rigid boundaries for cities, counties, countries, etc. But the Indigenous world view predates the drawing of boundaries and signing of deeds. They made distinctions based not on artificial boundaries drawn by surveyors, but on tradition, physical landmarks, and their own intimate knowledge of the land. To say the Meskwaki lived in Iowa is meaningless. These artificial boundaries were created by European settlers. The entire framework of land ownership since Columbus' first voyage has been shaped by what's known as the Doctrine of Discovery. In 1493, Pope Alexander VI issued an edict that territories occupied by non-Christians could be "discovered" and claimed for Christianity. Add to that the concept of *terra nullius*, a Latin expression meaning "land belonging to nobody," which colonialists used to lay claim to land that was not, in their opinion, being "used." To Europeans, this meant land that was being worked for agriculture and had permanent structures on it. Some Indigenous Nations, particularly in Central and South America, built permanent structures including temples and royal palaces, and numerous tribes throughout the Americas grew their own food. But many nations, especially those dependent on hunting, lived semi-nomadic, seasonally-based lifestyles, which didn't fit the European mold of permanent occupation.

Their biggest disadvantage, though, came from what Canadian author Ronald Wright calls the Europeans' "invisible weapons" – microbes to which the Indigenous peoples of the Americas had no natural immunity. Europeans wanted to believe that it was their innate superiority that allowed them to conquer the Americas, when it was actually a combination of biology and sheer dumb luck. The deadliest killer was smallpox, in which waves of epidemics wiped out entire populations in a matter of days. Historians believe that smallpox and other contagions are responsible for reducing the Indigenous population by as much as ninety percent in the early post-contact period. It wasn't just the death toll from the plagues themselves, but the fact that they often struck at critical points in Native people's battle against colonial encroachment. The question is as inevitable as it is – literally – unsettling: What might have been the outcome of European contact, if not for successive plagues that drastically reduced Indigenous populations and military might? What would the present-day map of the Americas look like?

In the early-nineteenth century, a string of treaties bolstered colonial efforts to establish settlements west of the Appalachians. But in 1830 the era of "no more nice (white) guy" was ushered in with the passage of the Indian Removal Act, under President

Andrew Jackson. The Act decreed what its name made abundantly clear, forcing all Indian nations east of the Mississippi River to surrender their lands. Through the following decade, dozens of tribes including the Cherokee, the Seminole, and the Choctaw were forcibly removed to present-day Oklahoma, then considered "Indian Territory." Known as the Trail of Tears, these forced relocations brought enormous hardship on Native Americans, with periods of starvation and outbreaks of disease and death.

A Shrinking Homeland

Historically, the Meskwaki were a semi-nomadic culture, electing to live together in a single, concentrated area during the summer months but scattering into smaller, independent areas throughout the winter season. The Meskwaki economy combined hunting, gathering, and agriculture and did not depend on one means or another exclusively. Some other tribes were primarily agrarian or hunting-based and if those pursuits were threatened, their entire community life was compromised. By comparison, the Meskwaki were not dependent on one single way of making a living and were thus more flexible in adapting to sudden changes that devastated many other tribes. This was definitely a factor in their ability to recover from the demographic catastrophe that was the Fox Wars. At the time of their war with the French, the Meskwaki regarded their homeland as the huge swath of land extending from Green Bay down the full length of the Fox River, an area that encompasses most of the present-day states of Wisconsin, Illinois and Iowa. There is ample historical evidence that the Meskwaki inhabited a large portion of eastern Iowa from the early 1700s to the present day. They were far from the only tribes in Iowa; there were also Sioux, Pottawatomi, Winnebago, Kickapoo, and the Ioway, who gave the state its name. What happened to the Meskwaki fits the familiar litany of broken promises, contested treaties and forced relocations that characterized the practices of the U.S. government from its earliest days. In a real sense, the Meskwaki had their own version of the Trail of Tears.

Their problems began with an 1804 Treaty between the government and the Sauk, which was hotly contested by the Meskwaki because they were not represented at the signing. The government officials ignored their protests and from then on treated the Sauk and Fox as one nation, as they still do to this day. Through the next series of treaties and removals, the Meskwaki were pushed westward, leaving behind their Illinois-side Mississippi River village sites at present-day Galena, Savanna, and Prairie Du Chien. By 1836, the Meskwaki had been forced to surrender many of their Mississippi River villages on the Iowa-side, sites that included present-day locales Dubuque, Iowa City, and Cedar Rapids. Some of the fiercest resistance to the government's relocation efforts came from the Meskwaki's near-cousins, the Sauk. In 1832, a group of more than a thousand Sauk men, women, and children led by the famous war chief Black Hawk crossed the Mississippi in an attempt to reclaim their village of Saukenuk, on the Illinois side. This move triggered the brief but bloody conflict known as the Black Hawk War. Black Hawk hoped that neighboring tribes like the Winnebago and the Kickapoo would join his followers, sparking a massive uprising of Indian nations against the United States. Some did, but for a variety of reasons, widespread support for his rebellion never materialized. Significantly, the Meskwaki, under the leadership of Chief Poweshiek, mostly stayed out of the conflict. After a series of increasingly bloody battles, government forces launched a final assault near the town of Victory, Wisconsin, which ended in a brutal massacre of elders, women, and children who were trying to flee across the Mississippi.

The Black Hawk War ended in 1833, concluding with a series of treaties and land transfers known collectively as the Black Hawk Purchase. This consisted of a large tract of land in eastern Iowa stretching more than fifty miles west of the Mississippi. Over the next few decades, through a series of government maneuvers, the Meskwaki and the Sauk watched the rest of their Iowa lands devoured by the advancing American frontier. In the end, it was the Treaty of 1842 that left the Meskwaki no choice but to leave their villages, gather at a site near present-day Des Moines, and await further removal to Kansas. In 1845, the U.S. government decreed that all prairie lands west of the Mississippi would be open to settlers, and the Meskwaki were finally forced to vacate the last of their lands in Iowa.

Or so government officials believed. Poweshiek's apparent compliance with the relocation policy masked a kind of stealth resistance. Some Meskwaki stayed behind, hiding in their old villages, while many of those who left for Kansas changed their minds and secretly journeyed back to the homeland. In point of fact, despite their agreement to evacuate the state within three years, the Meskwaki never really left Iowa. In 1846, the U.S. Cavalry were still finding and removing small bands of Meskwaki, but throughout the years following their banishment, they managed to maintain an unbroken presence in the state. In the 1850s, yet another forced displacement of their people to the Oklahoma territory was the last straw for the Meskwaki Nation. They decided to try and play the white man's game.

Under Chief Mamenwaneke, the Meskwaki launched what nowadays we might call a "charm offensive" on Iowa legislators. Despite the fact that in the nineteenth century Indians were not considered legal citizens and only U.S. citizens could own property, the tribe lobbied the state for permission to buy land. In 1856 their efforts paid off when the Iowa legislature passed a decree allowing them to buy a plot of land about fifty miles west of the city of Cedar Rapids. Over the next few years they managed to pool their meager government allotments to pay $735 cash for eighty acres in Tama County, named for a Meskwaki chief of the early-nineteenth century. The first group of Meskwaki to make their way back to Iowa was composed of eleven households, numbering about seventy-six individuals. A messenger was sent to other members of the tribe still living in hiding, to inform them about the land purchase, and urge them to join the main group at what would become the present-day Meskwaki settlement.

This unprecedented purchase of land turned out to be a brilliant move that changed the fortunes of the tribe forever. It's no small irony that they had to buy back their own land from a white farmer, but in fact they had a considerable number of allies among the settlers. A group of whites launched a petition to block the sale to the Meskwaki, but a majority of the settlers in the area refused to sign the petition, and it went nowhere. The federal government tried, without success, to force the tribe back to their previous residence, a reservation in Kansas. Instead even more Meskwakis moved to the Tama settlement. Ten years later, the U.S. government finally recognized the Meskwaki as the "Sac and Fox of the Mississippi in Iowa." For the next few decades, the tribe was largely ignored by various levels of government, with the result that the Meskwaki lived more independently than tribes confined to Indian reservations regulated by federal authority. The Iowa land purchase was a courageous act for the Meskwaki Nation, and proved to be a turning point in their history. It gave them cultural stability and a sense of pride at a time when most Native American tribes were facing the loss of their traditional homelands and lived under oppressive government policies.

The Settling of Buchanan County

"Just imagine this county in 1842—a vast expanse of rolling prairie like a mighty sea of green, whose wild untrammeled grasses billowed like ocean waves with every breeze, streams whose clear, rippling waters teeming with fish life, flowed peacefully and tranquilly on, undisturbed except for the occasional rhythmic dip of a paddle and the splash of a canoe, or when some dexterous, agile Indian landed a fine specimen of the finny tribe; natural wood lands, whose rank and luxuriant undergrowth was never trod except by some fleet-footed animal or some stealthy moccasined red man on the chase, whose only echoes were those of wild animals or the guttural speech or war-whoop of the Indian, a country whose only use was a habitat for wild animals and still wilder savages, who challenged the advance of civilization and fought the usurpers of what they deemed were their inalienable rights...Thus

did the pioneers of 1842 select this garden spot as an ideal on which to expend their efforts to assist Dame Nature in her well laid plan... The vast, waving prairies have given place to fenced and cultivated fields; roadways, bridges, houses, churches, schools, and towns dot the landscape. We have inherited all these material comforts from our forebears and those heroic pioneers who wisely selected this spot, Buchanan County, as their home-land."

The above passage, from a 1914 *History of Buchanan County, Iowa and Its People,* is an excellent illustration of the early settler mentality; the romanticizing of the prairie landscape, the lionizing of their white forebears, the seemingly benign view of the "moccasined red man," who nevertheless had the temerity to challenge "the advance of civilization." The passage ends with the extraordinary claim that the residents of Buchanan County have "inherited" the land not from the previous Indigenous inhabitants, but from the "heroic pioneers" who replaced them in the mid-nineteenth century.

When I learned that the present-day Meskwaki nation was based in Iowa, I was intrigued. As I said earlier in this book, I have roots in Iowa, on my father's side. When I was growing up, we used to come and visit the family farm in Buchanan County, just outside the town of Independence on the banks of the Wapsipinicon. I have relatives scattered all over this area, in the cities of Cedar Rapids, Dubuque, and in Galena, on the Illinois side of the Mississippi. It seemed fortuitous that Marie-Angelique and I would share common roots in this part of the world. Tama is only a little more than an hour's drive from Independence. Still, the settlement where they live now is but a fraction of their former territory. I was curious to find out more about how this part of Iowa grew and changed.

Part of what was to become Buchanan County was included in the initial 1833 Black Hawk Purchase. But there's a reason why the county history quoted above begins with the year 1842. It was the Treaty of 1842 that consolidated the remainder of the Black Hawk Purchase lands and sealed the "last chapter of the government's relation with (the Sac and Fox) in the present limits of the state of Iowa." In other words, 1842 marked the point of no return, when the land that would become Buchanan County passed definitively into non-Indigenous, i.e., white, hands.

The first white settler in the County was William Bennett, who built a log cabin on the shore of the Wapsipinicon in the village of Quasqueton, meaning "swift running water," a place traditionally frequented by many Native groups in the area. Quasqueton was a major destination for early settlers west of the Mississippi until 1837, when the county seat was established at the growing town of Independence, nine miles to the northwest. Place-naming was an act of considerable import for these early settlers. Independence received its name because the American July 4th holiday was coming up soon, while the county was named in honor of Pennsylvania Senator James Buchanan, who later became the fifteenth president of the United States. (It's also worth noting that the next county to the west is named for the Sauk leader Black Hawk.) Throughout the region, the government acquired land from the Native American tribes in return for promises of relocation, protection, and payment of tribal debts. Once the transfers were complete, the lands were surveyed and divided, at which point the government sold them to white settlers.

Buchanan County grew slowly at first. The 1846 census lists 149 residents, and two years later the population had only grown to 250. Still, local historians have carefully compiled lists of "firsts" in the county – first store (1842, proprietor remembered only as "Old Dick" who stocked the "best brand obtainable of Old Bourbon Whisky"); first post office (1845); first white child (Charles Kessler, born 1842 near Quasqueton). Through the 1840s there was a land rush in Iowa, with wave upon wave of settlers arriving mostly from New England and other parts of the U.S. These early settlers were overwhelmingly Protestant, chiefly Methodists and Presbyterians, which left an indelible mark on the character of the region that persists today. Scrolling through lists of early county officers and officials, we find a steady stream of (male) Anglo-Saxon names, many noting their membership in fraternal societies like the Odd Fellows and Freemasons.

The population of the county exploded during the 1850s, when foreign-born immigrants, chiefly from Germany and Ireland, began to arrive in great numbers. The Irish who came to the United States after 1947 were overwhelmingly poor, landless peasants. Their own homeland had been ravaged by the Great Potato Famine, and they came to America to escape starvation. It's estimated that more than a million Irish starved to death during the famine years, and another two million emigrated. The population of Ireland never recovered to its pre-famine numbers. The majority of famine refugees gravitated to New York, Boston, and other cities on the East Coast, while a smaller number moved on to the Midwest, to the growing city of Chicago and rural areas like Buchanan County. Those immigrants were the lucky ones. They not only survived the famine, they had enough money to pay for their ship passage across the Atlantic.

Nowadays it's hard to believe that only a few generations ago, the Irish were an oppressed minority in America. They were simultaneously accused of stealing all the good jobs and branded as lazy and shiftless. The American media propagated the idea that the Irish were the non-white "missing link" between the superior European and the savage African. In the popular press, the Irish were depicted as subhuman; carriers of disease; unclean, drunken brawlers, who wallowed in crime and bred like rats. Added to this toxic mix was the fact that most famine refugees were Roman Catholics coming to an overwhelmingly Protestant nation, where their fealty to the Pope made their allegiance to the United States suspect. Though they eventually assimilated into the mainstream, for much of the nineteenth century the Irish were subjected to racial and anti-immigrant discrimination. In places like Buchanan County, these attitudes were overlaid with the anti-Catholic prejudice shared by the overwhelmingly white, largely Protestant Europeans who preceded them.

Throughout their history the Irish, like black people and the Indigenous peoples of the Americas, suffered under British colonial rule. This is not at all to suggest they were as equally oppressed as those groups. A recurring meme on the Internet – that the Irish were brought to America as slaves and had it as bad as, or worse than, blacks – is patently false. But Frederick Douglass, the great leader of the abolitionist movement, saw parallels between the plight of the Irish and his fellow blacks, and wrote about them in his memoirs. Douglass witnessed first-hand the horrific beginnings of the famine on his 1845 speaking tour through Ireland; a life-changing experience that created a bond with the Irish people that lasted throughout his long life. Some Indigenous nations also expressed feelings of kinship with the Irish. One of the most extraordinary acts of the mid-nineteenth century was the Choctaw Nation's donation to the famine victims of Cork. Having only recently survived the forced march of the Trail of Tears themselves, the Choctaw felt a deep empathy with Ireland's famine victims. In the midst of their own poverty and hardship, they collected $170 (over $10,000 in today's dollars) from their members and sent it to Cork in 1847. The bond between the Choctaw and the Irish remains strong to the present day, and in 2017, a remarkable memorial sculpture, "Kindred Spirits" was unveiled in Midleton, a suburb of Cork.

Still, alongside the desperate circumstances of the famine refugees sits the uncomfortable fact that the Irish, like all settlers, are interlopers in North America, the beneficiaries of the U.S. government's seizure of Indigenous lands. I was, of course, well acquainted with that general fact when I started researching Marie-Angelique's life. But when I saw the 19th-century map of Buchanan County with the farm plots marked "Burns" and "McDonnell," I realized I had some genealogical research of my own to do. Fortunately, I didn't have to start from scratch. One of my cousins had done some initial searching (back when the World Wide Web was just a gleam in WWW creator Tim Berners-Lee's eye) and I was able to build on her work. Here's the narrative I was able to put together:

In 1858, a year after the Meskwaki purchase of the land in Tama, an Irish immigrant named James Burns brought his family from County Armagh, including his sixteen-year-old son John, to the United States. James purchased farmland in Buchanan County near the village of Quasqueton. A few years later, John Burns bought his own farm plot about ten miles northwest, near the growing town of Independence, for $7.50 an acre. John Burns married Mary Jane Glynn, whose family hailed from County Clare in Ireland, and they raised ten children on the farm. The *History of Buchanan County* speaks highly of John Burns as one of its pioneers: "He is a man of clear grit and stout heart, and has won by his own exertions a splendid farm and good home… From the age of sixteen years he has resided continuously in Buchanan county and has, therefore, witnessed much of its growth and development through a period of more than a half-century."

Another Irish couple, John and Bridget McDonnell, fled famine-ravaged County Mayo for England in 1847. Along with many other Irish immigrants, they eked out a living for a few years in the industrial Midlands around Birmingham, but ultimately left for America in search of a better life. They made their way to Iowa where, in 1871, they bought a plot of land adjacent to the Burns' farm. There they lived out their lives, growing crops, tending livestock, and raising their seven children, one of whom, James, married John and Mary Jane Burns' daughter Sarah. James and Sarah had thirteen children, of whom my father, Alfred, was third eldest.

James McDonnell and Sarah Burns were my paternal grandparents.

Like the majority of residents of the North American continent, I am descended from the Europeans who displaced the original inhabitants. The Meskwaki people lived, hunted, and fished in this part of eastern Iowa over which my relatives are scattered. I am not only a settler, but a direct descendant of people who settled on the traditional lands of Marie-Angelique's people.

I was intrigued when I first became aware of this ancestral connection with Marie-Angelique's people. The Meskwaki presence in eastern Iowa dates at least as far back as the early-eighteenth century. I began to entertain the idea that there might be a sort of spiritual bond between the two of us that transcended time and space. Could the young child Marie-Angelique have come with her family to a winter campsite in what is now Buchanan County? Could she have gathered swan potatoes on the banks of the Wapsie River with her mother? Could she once have walked there, on the very spot where my grandparents' farm stood?

It's not impossible. But it's pretty much beside the point, especially when set against the yawning gap between our respective lives. My Irish ancestors had to leave their homeland to survive. But because they were of European origin, they had a place – America – to flee to. The Indigenous peoples were living in America when Europeans arrived. Over the next few centuries their homelands were stolen from them, piece by piece, treaty by treaty, war by war. But unlike the Irish diaspora, there was no "New World" for them to go to. The result was genocidal and assimilationist policies that drastically reduced their populations and nearly destroyed their cultures. By 1860, every inch of the state of Iowa had passed from Native to non-Native ownership – with one notable exception: the settlement in Tama. The Meskwaki were – *are* – the last tribe of Iowa.

CHAPTER 12

Lost Daughter of the Red Earth People

Iowa, January 2018

The Meskwaki Bingo Casino Hotel is a mammoth, multi-building complex that dominates the view from U.S. 30, historically known as the Lincoln Highway. Alec and I are in Tama County, about an hour's drive west of Cedar Rapids, on the way to the Meskwaki Cultural Center and Museum. We stop to ask for directions and learn that we missed the turnoff to the museum, which is at the eastern end of the settlement. We drive back to the turnoff, where I get my first view of the residential community. It strikes me as low-key, almost suburban, dotted with a few official buildings and dozens of tidy houses with lots of space in between.

The museum is housed in a modest-sized, single-story building; a former daycare center. It is beautifully designed, softly lit, and full of handmade crafts – carvings, weaving, intricate beading – and displays chronicling tribal history. In the middle of the room sits what looks like a massive, rotting log. The accompanying plaque says that it is, in fact, the remnants of a 250-year-old dugout canoe. The dates don't line up exactly, but I look at it thinking that as a child Marie-Angelique was probably carried in a vessel much like this.

The museum and cultural center, which opened in 2010, is largely the work of Johnathan Buffalo, the tribe's director of Historical Preservation. I've read quite a few of his articles online and seen his impressive list of academic credentials. I'd spoken to him on the phone a few weeks earlier and mentioned that I had family living not far from the settlement. At the time, it seemed an innocuous comment. But since then I'd learned much more about my ancestors and the specific lands they had settled on. Now I was unnerved. How would I be received? Would he regard me as just another settler; a clueless white lady? Not to mention that, as a Canadian, I almost feel like I should apologize for the Fox Wars.

In our earlier phone conversation, I'd introduced myself and explained the purpose of my call. I told him about my trip to France and the *Exposition* I'd attended. As we spoke it became clear that he had some familiarity with Marie-Angelique's story, and that Aroles' conclusion that she was of Fox origin wasn't news to him. I mentioned that the organizers of the *Exposition* had expressed interest in learning more about where Marie-Angelique had come from and who her people were and had raised the possibility of making contact with the Meskwaki Nation. I said that I'd volunteered to act as liaison, since the organizers didn't speak English well. I paused, waiting for his response, which took me aback.

"You know, the French have never apologized to our people for what they did to us."

"No," I agreed. "They haven't."

I realized that he was talking about the Fox Wars. I hastened to explain that the people I'd met in France very much regretted what had happened to Marie-Angelique. They wanted to know if there was some way they could make amends for it.

Johnathan Buffalo was having none of it. "We have not forgotten."

He went on, in a somewhat goading, but playful tone. "When we watch movies about World War II where the Nazis are fighting the French, do you know who we're cheering for?"

"I think I can guess."

He grew more serious as he went on to explain the deep – he didn't hesitate to use the word "hatred" – that the Meskwaki people harbor for the French nation. "We're glad they got driven out of North America," he said. "We figure we won the war. Look, we're still here, and there's no more French king."

After looking around the museum a bit, I approached the information desk and asked if it would be possible for me to speak the director. I hadn't made an appointment, but the woman at the desk seemed nonplussed. She said that he was with someone at the moment, and would I mind waiting a few minutes? "Of course not," I replied. I could hear a murmur of conversation from the office just opposite her desk. A few minutes later, a man came out of the office, leaving the door open. The woman at the desk nodded to me to go in. I paused tentatively at the doorway, waiting for him to notice me, and then stepped into the office and introduced myself.

"Mr. Buffalo? I'm Kathleen McDonnell, from Canada. We spoke on the phone a few weeks ago."

No reaction.

I continued, "The one writing about Marie-Angelique, the girl who was taken to France."

That seemed to click. He nodded and gestured toward the chair opposite his desk. I started off by telling him how moved and impressed I was by the museum displays, a strategic compliment that also happened to be true. We covered some of the same ground as our earlier conversation – Aroles' research into Marie-Angelique's background, how the French were shocked that a young woman could climb a tree. I took pains to stress that there was no way to attain certainty about information that was nearly three centuries old, and thus no conclusive proof that Marie-Angelique was Fox. Personally, I told him, I'd come to the conclusion that Aroles' research was valid, that she very likely was of Fox / Meskwaki heritage.

There was a pause in the conversation. So far, he had been perfectly cordial, but I was still anxious.

After a few moments of silence, he spoke. "The one thing I would say is this. There were people who wondered what happened to this person. There were people who wanted to know where she was and whether she was all right."

I hastened to agree with him. Yes, that was one of the reasons I wanted to write about her, to try and help fill in the story of her life before she was taken from North America. Like Serge Aroles, Isabelle Guyot, and so many others, I felt driven to do what I could to restore Marie-Angelique to history.

He went on to talk about the many Meskwaki lives lost during the Fox Wars and later conflicts, speaking of these losses as if they had happened yesterday, rather than centuries ago. "This person had people who cried for her," he said. "She is one of our lost babies."

All I could do was nod silently in agreement.

After another pause, he posed a question to me. "Does anyone know where this person is buried?"

I was relieved to be able to give him information he didn't already know, which I'd only recently become aware of myself. I replied that she had originally been buried in a churchyard in Paris back in 1775. But in the early-nineteenth century, the cemeteries in Paris had become dangerously overcrowded and many had to be shut down, including the cemetery of St. Nicholas des Champs, where Marie-Angelique was buried. Her skeletal remains were deposited in the vast ossuary known as the catacombs, where they are now mixed in among the bones of six million other Parisians. There is no longer a burial site, no headstone, for the Wild Girl.

I asked if the tribe might consider some symbolic way of bringing her home.

He shook his head. "That's not necessary. She gets a Free Pass."

I looked confused. Free Pass?

He explained that in Meskwaki spiritual tradition, certain rites must be carried out during the four-day period after death, to ensure that the deceased is reunited with family, loved ones, and ancestors in the spirit world. If the rituals can't be carried out because of war, accident, or other factors, that requirement is waived. Hence the Free Pass. The child taken from her homeland all those centuries ago, Johnathan assured me, now resides with her family and the rest of her ancestors.

"She is a Meskwaki spirit now." He said this with a calm certitude that was reassuring. There was no concern that Marie-Angelique was some kind of wandering spirit, trapped in the piles of bones under the city of Paris.

I asked what he thought the Meskwaki people would feel about an outsider, a non-Native person, writing about Marie-Angelique. The question didn't seem to concern him very much. She is now known by a name in a foreign language, and her story had unfolded in far-flung parts of the world. His conviction that her spirit had been reunited with her Meskwaki ancestors rendered those considerations irrelevant.

As Johnathan escorted us out of the museum, we encountered a woman coming out of the adjacent building. Johnathan introduced us to her – his wife, Suzanne Wanatee Buffalo, who worked next door in the tribal courthouse, where she served as deputy clerk. I also knew she was a member of the Iowa State Indian Advisory Council and had herself written extensively on Meskwaki history. I could see right away that she was a powerful woman, a formidable presence in the community, and that she and her husband were what people like to call a power couple.

Suzanne was on a break and didn't have long to talk, so we stood outside in the brisk January air while I told her about my book project. She said she wasn't surprised to learn that Marie-Angelique, a woman with such a strong will to survive, was Meskwaki. "You take a Meskwaki woman and put her anywhere on this earth and she'll figure it all out. She'll survive."

As Alec and I drove back to the highway, I thought about what I'd learned in Catholic school about infants who died before they could be baptized. The nuns had taught us that these babies still bore the stain of Original Sin on their souls, and had to go to a place called "Limbo" and wait – maybe for all eternity! – in hopes that one day God would let them into Heaven. As an adult, I learned that Infant Limbo is not an official Church doctrine. But as kids we believed everything the nuns taught us, and the idea of Limbo didn't sit well with me and my friends. It wasn't the babies' fault they weren't baptized! A truly merciful, just God would do like the Meskwaki and give those innocents a Free Pass into Heaven.

There is no place I belong in this world…

The words I had put into the character Marie-Angelique's mouth came back to me. It occurred to me that I might have been completely mistaken. Maybe there was a place where she belonged. Maybe there still is – here, with the other lost daughters of the Red Earth People.

CHAPTER 13
Marie-Angelique was Here

Paris, October 2018

I'm standing at the intersection of rue du Temple and rue Notre-Dame du Nazareth, near the northern edge of the Marais District in the 2nd *arrondissement*. Just a stone's throw away is the bustling Place de la Republique, one of those vast public squares that dot the city of Paris. Once a busy traffic roundabout ruled by the car, it underwent a radical transformation a few years ago into a pedestrian plaza with a café and an array of wooden seating platforms, which the skateboarders make enthusiastic use of. Looming over the plaza is an enormous bronze statue of "Marianne," the national symbol of the French Republic, surrounded by representations of the guiding spirits of the 1789 revolution: *liberté, égalité, fraternité*. Marianne and her companion statues weren't here, of course, when Marie-Angelique died in a nearby apartment, more than a decade before the revolution.

Somewhere on this spot, where rue du Temple meets rue Notre-Dame du Nazareth, is the place Marie-Angelique lived out her final years, after she'd become an independently wealthy woman. There are rows of three- and four-storey apartment buildings on both sides of the street. They don't look that old, but in Paris, it's hard to tell. On the north side of the street is an iron gate with a decorative stone arch that looks like it could have been here in 1775. But either way, I know I'm near the patch of planet Earth where the Wild Girl lived and died.

Marie-Angelique was here.

I don't have the same degree of certainty about the other address I'm going to check out. Which is surprising, because it's noted very specifically in the historical record. In James Burnett's preface to the 1768 English translation of Mme. Hequet's biography of *La Fille Sauvage*, he announced her co-ordinates for all the world to see: "For the satisfaction of any readers of this pamphlet who may happen to be in Paris, and have the curiosity of paying a visit to Mademoiselle LeBlanc, I here give her address in the year 1765: *Rue St. Antoine vis à vis la rue vielle du Temple sur la troisieme etage sur le Devant* ['St. Antoine Street nearly opposite Old Temple Street on the third floor in the front']." You'd think it couldn't get more precise than that, but there's a problem – rue St. Antoine doesn't intersect with rue du vielle Temple, at least it doesn't nowadays. I suspect it might have something to do with changing street names over the centuries, which also leads me to wonder whether "rue du vielle Temple" is the same as the one now called "rue vielle du Temple." I figure the best thing to do is to head south on rue du vielle Temple, toward the river. It's an unseasonably warm October afternoon, so I stop at the Café des Philosophes for an espresso, sipping it at an outside table where a nearby busker is playing "Hello Dolly" on a trumpet. I continue south, and shortly before reaching the river I cross rue de Rivoli, a wide street lined with boutiques. I note on the map that a few blocks to the west, the name of Rivoli changes to St. Antoine.

In the past few days, Alec and I have re-visited Songy and Chalons-en-Champagne, watching from the train as we pass vast fields of canola, beets, and *éoliennes*. It turns out that, economically, things might be looking up for the region: Chalons is getting a brand-new jail, which is expected to create quite a few new jobs. But as we learn from the Phelizons, it was a tough year for winemakers: As a result of a summer-long drought, the grapes are too sweet, and will have to be mixed with juice from previous vintages. To my taste, the champagne they serve us at lunch is as exquisite as ever.

Of course, I have a swim in the moat, and we walk across the field to the *l'Ile de la Fille Sauvage*, which seems even more eerily silent than I remember. When we were last here, there was talk of building a proper walkway with signage from the entrance of the winery to the *Ile*. But there's been no movement on that front, largely due to the further deterioration of relations between the Phelizons and the mayor. Eric and Marie-Ange recount with indignation Mayor Passinhas' recent efforts to trademark the phrase *La Fille Sauvage* for tourism purposes. I have to admit that the idea sounds pretty ridiculous. I don't know anything about French law, but surely one can't claim ownership of a string of words in common use. And we agree that the Wild Girl's story should be considered part of the common heritage of the area, not the property of a single village. Two things are clear. There is still no flood of tourists, not even a trickle, to Songy. And the rivalry between *le vigneron* and *le maire* isn't going to end any time soon.

Yet, in the wider world of Wild Girl *aficionados*, things appear to be settling down. The *Exposition* has been displayed in a number of French towns in the past year-and-a-half, but its final booking is coming up soon, though Isabelle Guyon still has hopes that it might travel outside France. Last year Julia Douthwaite published an intriguing piece in a collection of French essays. "*La Jeune Fille Sauvage Mis a Jour et Quelques Avenues pour l'Avenir*" expanded on her previous work, exploring the role of racism and colonialism in creating the "legend" of the Wild Girl. In 2018, though, Douthwaite retired from her academic post at the University of Notre Dame, took her married surname, and moved back to her hometown, Seattle, where she started an online business, Honey Girl Books and Gifts. As for Franck Rolin, aka Serge Aroles, he too appears to have withdrawn from the Marie-Angelique universe, at least for the moment. He is continuing his medical relief work in Ethiopia, where he now lives full-time with a new wife and son.

As I've said throughout this book, my own relationship to Marie-Angelique has undergone a transition. Since I decided to put aside the play I was writing about her, she is no longer "my" character. I've come back to Paris to make a kind of pilgrimage, to honor the fact that she was a living person who walked these streets and breathed the air of Paris. I have one more stop on my itinerary, though, and my feelings about this one are complicated.

The Empire of Death

Among the many crimes committed against Indigenous peoples by their colonial usurpers was the theft of their art and sacred objects. In Canada, the holdings of prominent institutions like the Royal Ontario Museum and the Glenbow Museum are full of artifacts taken from Indigenous nations over the centuries. Here and elsewhere, the idea of "repatriation," the practice of returning these artifacts to their original owners, has gained currency as an acknowledgement of Europeans' historic role in the erasure of Indigenous heritage. And the practice doesn't only apply to artifacts; in some cases, it even includes human remains of individuals who, like Marie-Angelique, were stolen from their communities of origin.

Take the famous case of Abraham Ulrikab, who in 1880 was taken to Europe along with seven other Labrador Inuit, where they were exhibited in so-called Human Zoos. A year later they were all dead from smallpox, which they had not been vaccinated against. In 2010, a Quebec researcher named France Rivet set out to locate Ulrikab's remains, which she finally traced to the Muséum National d'Histoire Naturelle in Paris. The museum agreed to return Ulrikab's remains to Labrador, and the Inuit are currently in discussions with French authorities as to how this repatriation will be carried out.

According to Serge Aroles, Marie-Angelique was buried on the grounds of the Church of St. Nicholas-des-Champs, which according to the historical record was one of the cemeteries that was dug up and moved to the catacombs. I assumed that this meant that physical repatriation would not be an option for her remains, but now I wonder. Was that really the case? I knew almost nothing about the catacombs, other than the fact that the remains of an estimated six million Parisians were down there. That's an awful lot of bones, but how were they situated? Were they just in random piles? I decided I had to look into it further.

By the late eighteenth-century, the cemeteries of the growing city were bursting at the seams. A great many of the bodies hadn't been buried properly and were spreading disease. Parisian officials decided to condemn the city's burial grounds and move the remains they contained elsewhere, turning to the city's maze of underground quarries. Over several decades they were able to organize the movement of bodies from previously existing graveyards, transporting the dead via carts to the underground quarries. Today the more than six million deceased Parisians in the catacombs include figures like Robespierre and Danton, who were guillotined during the revolution. Although the ossuary comprises only a small section of the underground network of tunnels, Parisians commonly refer to the entire tunnel network as *Les Catacombes*.

The catacombs have been open for public visitation since the late-nineteenth century, and since then an entire mythology has sprung up around what's been called the "Empire of Death." The Phantom of the Opera and *Les Miserables*' Jean Valjean both haunted these tunnels. During World War II, the invading Nazi army occupied a bunker in the tunnels below the 6th *arrondisement*. Striking students descended into the catacombs during the 1968 student uprising. In 2004, an entire cinema was discovered sixty feet beneath the city, including a bar, lounge, and a screening area where twenty seats had been carved into the stone. Officials chalked the finding up to a clandestine group of "cataphiles," daredevils and urban explorers who delight in the forbidden; in breaking the rules. There's even a group of outlaw swimmers who take occasional dips in the tunnels' underground pools. (Yes, I was tempted. But I didn't manage to make contact with the group. I did, however, connect with a Facebook group called Paris Wild Swimming, and joined a few of them for an outlaw swim in the *Canal de l'Ourcq*. I like to think that Marie-Angelique would have approved.)

In their first years, the catacombs were a disorganized bone repository. In the early-nineteenth century, Louis-Étienne Héricart de Thury, director of Mines Inspection, oversaw extensive renovations that transformed the underground caverns into a veritable mausoleum, with thousands of skulls and femurs arranged in patterns on the walls and in the walkways, an arrangement that survives to this day. So, the ossuaries in the catacombs were not random, but organized in some fashion. Still, I wanted to know more.

I turned to – where else? – Google, which offered up a slew of amateur videos of walks through the catacombs. Most were short, but I found the motherlode in a video that had amassed nearly 200,000 views. The video, posted by a user who goes by the moniker "Lättsmält," begins with a walk through a long tunnel – so long that after a minute or so, Lättsmält thoughtfully fast-forwards through to the ossuaries. As the camera wends its way through the tunnels the viewer periodically encounters signage indicating the origin of each collection of bones. Frustratingly, Lättsmält didn't pause long enough at any one sign to allow me to read the text. Until, remarkably, at the twelve-minute mark, the camera lingers on one of the signs just long enough to allow me to make out the writing, though I need a magnifying glass to do it. (I've said before that this search for the Wild Girl had elements of a detective story, which was now becoming literally true.)

"Ossemens du Cimitiere St. Nicholas des Champs. Le 24 Août 1804."

The date was right. It seemed almost too perfect. There on the screen I saw row upon row of neatly-stacked bones with a layer of skulls on top. Could it be that somewhere in that very stack were the bones of the Wild Girl? Was it possible that I could go into the catacombs myself, find my way to this section, and stand within inches of her physical remains?

It was another of those moments that I'd had since I'd begun working on this book. At every point, it seemed, I'd found just the information I needed. At times it felt like I was being led by something outside myself, that the pieces were coming to me unbidden – almost as if I was being summoned by... what? The spirit of Marie-Angelique herself? Once again, it was time to cue the *Twilight Zone* theme music...

When I had been planning the trip to Paris, I'd had every intention of making the trek through the catacombs, to see if I could locate the *Ossemens du Cimitiere St. Nicholas des Champs*.

But as the time grew closer, I found myself questioning the whole idea. Why did I want to do this? Was it a respectful thing to do? For Indigenous people, the burial grounds of their ancestors are sacred places that should not be disturbed. In North America, Native people raise objections when land developers and archeologists plan to dig up known burial sites, and increasingly these objections are being honored and accommodated by various levels of government. But a mass grave that doubles as a tourist attraction? The more I thought about it, it was hard to imagine a situation more at odds with the Meskwaki world-view. When I'd spoken to Johnathan Buffalo about the catacombs, he'd displayed little discernable reaction. I began to wonder what he would think of my plan to visit what was the likely repository of Marie-Angelique's bones.

In the end, the decision was made for me. It turned out the one day I'd set aside for my Paris walkabout was a Monday, and on Mondays the catacombs were closed to the public. I was relieved, actually. I realized I wasn't at all eager to venture down into the Empire of Death. But I still wanted to do something to pay my respects. Since an ossuary is basically a cemetery without headstones, I decided that going to the entrance to the catacombs would be the equivalent of visiting a gravesite in a cemetery.

I took the Metro, got off at Denfert-Rochereau station, and looked around. The paper map and Google both indicated that the entrance to the catacombs should be right there, clearly visible. There was some signage, but there was a busy traffic circle opposite the station, making it hard to tell which way the arrows were pointing – at least for someone as directionally challenged as I am. I wandered the area for several minutes and was almost ready to give up when I stopped to ask a man selling roasted chestnuts. I'd barely gotten a word out when he pointed directly across from his corner to a white building surrounded by hoardings. I crossed the street for what was now the fourth time. Sure enough, there it was, the entrance almost completely hidden, with a small sign: *Les Catacombes de Paris.*

I sat down facing the locked iron gate. After a few moments, I could feel my frustration fading away, replaced by a wave of quiet sadness. The words of Johnathan Buffalo came into my mind.

She is a Meskwaki spirit now.

Swimming under the Bridges

Leaving the catacombs, I boarded the Metro again and got off at St. Michel, so I could walk across the river on my way back to the Marais. I failed to factor in that it was the station closest to Notre-Dame, and soon found myself in the square adjacent to the cathedral, surrounded by a swarm of tourists.

I circled around the crowds and headed for the Pont St. Louis, one of the few pedestrian-only bridges that cross the river in the heart of the city. The bridge was nearly empty, and the quiet was a welcome respite from the bustle of Notre-Dame. I started making my way to the top. Because the Pont St. Louis connects two islands – Ile de la Cité and Ile Saint-Louis – at some points it's possible to look around and see the grand sweep of bridges on both channels of the river.

I was reminded of my time in Ireland a couple of years earlier, when I took part in the Dublin City Liffey Swim. It's an open-water swimming event that's coming up to its 100th year in 2019. (Those who find the thought of swimming in an urban river distasteful, you may want to stop reading here.) The Liffey Swim is a race, but most of the participants do it as a lark, for fun and the satisfaction of finishing the 2-km. course. The year I did it, there were more than 400 swimmers, entering the river from pontoons in separate men's and women's heats. The women have a tradition of singing the opening lines of a beloved folk tune as they plunge into the river.

> *In Dublin's fair city, where the girls are so pretty*
> *'Twas there that I met my sweet Molly Malone*
> *She drove her wheelbarrow through the streets broad and narrow*
> *Singing "cockles and mussels, alive, alive, oh."*

I didn't know any of the women in my heat, but their camaraderie was infectious. What made it truly exhilarating was the sensation of swimming under the Liffey bridges – nine in all – to the cheers of the crowds gathered on both banks of the river. It was one of the most memorable swimming experiences of my life. Now, standing on the Pont St. Louis, I recalled the scene in my play where I'd imagined Marie-Angelique doing the very same thing.

> *Crowds gathered along the banks of the Seine when a woman was sighted in the river near the Pont Marie. "Look," they shouted. "Someone has fallen into the water!" But she refused all offers of help or rescue and began to swim downriver. People stood watching on the bridge or ran along the banks, thinking she must surely be mad, or so despondent as to take her own life. A gendarme was alerted and shouted to her to swim over to the right bank where she could be pulled from the water. But she ignored him and kept on swimming toward the Pont Notre-Dame.*
>
> *People were astounded. They had never seen such behavior in a woman. They kept expecting that she would tire of swimming and slip beneath the surface. But remarkably, her strokes grew stronger and stronger. She passed under the Pont Au Change, and by the time she reached the Pont Neuf, something astonishing occurred. The people standing on each bridge began to cheer her on as she swam underneath. "Keep going!" they cried. "Keep going!"*
>
> *And so she did. She swam under the Pont Royal and on toward the outskirts of the city. She kept on swimming, and swimming, and swimming. Until she could be seen no more.*

During her lifetime, Marie-Angelique never really knew where she came from. When I wrote that passage, I had only a vague idea where she might be going. From Paris the Seine flows northwesterly for 120 miles, where it meets the English Channel and empties into the Atlantic Ocean. It's an awfully long way to go.

Swim Home

But at least now I know where she's headed. In my thoughts I cheer her on.

Keep going, lost daughter of the Red Earth People.
Swim home.

Unnamed Meskwaki child, early 20th century
From the collection of Meskwaki Cultural Center and Museum
Used with permission

NOTES ON SOURCES

The experience of researching and writing this book has been a bit like a scavenger hunt, with no clear goal and many wrong turns. When I first did a Google search of "Marie-Angelique," among the first hits that came up were a fortune-teller in France and a bra fitting specialist in Missouri. I also had to be wary of sources confusing Marie-Angelique LeBlanc with a different, similarly-named historical person. Marie-Joseph Angelique was a black slave living in Montreal (yes, there were enslaved blacks in early Canada). She was charged with arson and executed in 1734 – another little-known story of a woman oppressed by colonialism.

In researching *Swim Home*, I found myself going to unexpected places, tracking down sources and texts that I had no idea existed. It was the journey itself that dictated the steps, the pace. It wasn't about me, it was about uncovering the truth of another life, and the sense of responsibility that came with that. It was an exhilarating adventure, one that I want to share with the readers of this book – not in the form of academic footnotes, but with references that allow you to further explore on your own.

The quote about swimming on the opening page is from *The Autobiography of a Fox Indian Woman*, published in the 40th Annual Report Bureau of American Ethnology to the Secretary of the Smithsonian Institution for the Years 1918-1919, page 297. The woman agreed to dictate her childhood recollections to a translator, but made clear that she did not want her name published. Her reminiscences were then compiled and edited by Truman Michelson, a linguist and anthropologist.

CHAPTER 1

The legend of "Wapsi" and "Pinicon" can be found here: https://www.buchanancountyhistory.com/legendofthewapsi.php

CHAPTER 2

The *Mercure de France* was a French gazette and literary magazine that began publishing in the mid-17th century.

The major source about Marie-Angelique during her own lifetime was Mme. Hecquet's *An Account of a Savage Girl Caught Wild in the Woods of Champagne,* translated from the French by William Robertson, with a Preface by James Burnett, Lord Monboddo, Edinburgh, 1768. Burnett notes that his edition includes "Several Particulars that were Omitted in the Original Account."

The story of the so-called Monkey Girl was widely reported in international media in 2017. The *Guardian* was my source for the quotes "Eat mutton" and from Ranjana Kumari: https://www.theguardian.com/world/2017/apr/08/indian-girl-found-in-jungle-was-not-living-with-monkeys-officials-say

For this chapter, my main source was Michael Newton's *Savage Girls and Wild Boys: A History of Feral Children,* Macmillan, 2002. Other sources cited in Chapter 2 are listed below:

Ashley Montagu's review appears in *American Anthropologist,* vol. 45, 1943, 468-472.

Bruno Bettelheim, "Feral Children and Autistic Children" in *American Journal of Sociology* Vol. 64, No. 5 (Mar., 1959), 455-467.

Blake Eskin, "Crying Wolf: Why did it take so long for a far-fetched Holocaust memoir to be debunked?" *Slate*, Feb. 9, 2008. http://www.slate.com/articles/arts/culturebox/2008/02/crying_wolf.html

The opening lines of Aroles' *L'Enigme des enfants-loups* state his belief that "la forêt fut le vaste orphelinat de l'histoire de l'humanité." My own characterization of him as debunker-in-chief notwithstanding, it's clear that he also intended his book to tear away the veil of myth and folklore surrounding the historical fact of child abandonment. In that sense, his work is a companion to John Boswell's groundbreaking history of child abandonment: *The Kindness of Strangers: The Abandonment of Children in Western Europe from Late Antiquity to the Renaissance*. New York: Pantheon Books, 1988.

Under the Red and Yellow Stars, by Alex Levin. Azrieli Series of Holocaust Survivor Memoirs published by Second Story Press, Toronto. 2009.

CHAPTER 4

There are many references on Internet sites to Burnett's family connection with Robert Burns, including a well-known 1786 painting by James Edgar of Burns attending an evening party at Monboddo's house.

"Monboddo: The Enlightenment Man," a musical commissioned by Burnett's descendants, was mounted in Aberdeen in 2011.

Thomas M. Carr Jr., "The Quebec Hospitalière and the Closeted Jansenist: The Duplessis-Hecquet Correspondence," in *Canadian Society for Eighteenth-Century Studies* Volume 29, 2010.

Burnett discussed Huron languages and Peter of Hanover in his *Of the Origin and Progress of Language,* published in 6 volumes between 1773–1792.

CHAPTER 5

Memmie LeBlanc: A Play by Hilary Bell. https://australianplays.org/script/ASC-1048

La Fille Sauvage de Songy, a novel by Anne Cayre, L'Amourier Editions, Couraze, France, 2013.

For discussion of the Fox Wars in this and subsequent chapters, I drew on the following sources:

Brett Rushforth, "Slavery, Fox Wars and the Limitations of Alliance", in *The William and Mary Quarterly*, Vol. 63, No. 1, January, 2006, 53-80.

Bonds of Alliance: Indigenous and Atlantic Slaveries in New France, by Brett Rushforth, University of North Carolina Press, 2012.

The Fox Wars: The Mesquakie Challenge to New France, by R. David Edmunds and, Joseph L. Peyser University of Oklahoma Press, 2014.

There is a listing for Pierre-Gratien Martel de Brouague and other members of his family in the online *Dictionary of Canadian Biography*. Acoutsina also has an entry in the DCB.

This project gave me the opportunity to familiarize myself with the trail-blazing work of Quebec historian Marcel Trudel. I consulted two of his many books: *Canada's Forgotten Slaves: Two Hundred Years of Bondage* (originally published as: *Deux siècles d'esclavage au Québec*), translation by George Tombs, Montreal: Vehicule Press, 2013; and *Dictionnaire des esclaves et de leurs propriétaires au Canada français*, (A dictionary of Slaves and their Owners in French Canada), La Salle, Quebec: Hurtubise HMH, 1994.

The assessments of Aroles' conclusions by various scholars of Indigenous history dates from the late nineties and appears on a discussion board, H-Net, operated by Michigan State University: https://lists.h-net.org/cgi-bin/logbrowse.pl?trx=vx&list=H-AmIndian&month=9904&week=d&msg=yEPdHxq/U5SKjMkxikvVkg&user=&pw=

Julia V. Douthwaite, "Rewriting the Savage: The extraordinary fictions of the Wild Girl of Champagne" in *Eighteenth-Century Studies,* V. 28, No. 2, 1994, 163-192.

The Wild Girl, Natural Man and the Monster: Dangerous Experiments in the Age of Enlightenment by Julia V. Douthwaite, University of Chicago Press, 2002.

CHAPTER 6

Sauvage: Biographie de Marie-Angélique LeBlanc 1712-1775 by Aurélie Bévière, Jean-David Morvan, and Gaëlle Hersent, Paris: Delcourt, 2015.

CHAPTER 7

The Village Effect: How Face-to-Face Contact Can Make Us Healthier and Happier, by Susan Pinker, Penguin Random House / Vintage Canada 2015.

The quotes by Serge Aroles are taken from various emails to me and ones I was copied on.

CHAPTER 8

Island of the Blue Dolphins by Scott O'Dell, Houghton Mifflin, 1960.

Emma Hardacre, "Eighteen Years Alone: A Tale of the Pacific." in *Scribner's Monthly* 20, no. 5 1880, 657–64.

Emma Hardacre, "The Lone Woman of San Nicolas Island" in *The California Indians: Source Book*, edited by R. F. Heizer and M. A. Whipple. Berkeley: University of California Press, 1971, 272-281.

Handbook of the Indians of California, A. L. Kroeber, U.S. Government publications, 1925.

"A Critical Look at O'Dell's *Island of the Blue Dolphins*" Debbie Reese June 16, 2016: https://americanindiansinchildrensliterature.blogspot.com/2016/06/a-critical-look-at-odells-island-of.html

CHAPTER 9

The Myth of the Savage and the Beginnings of French Colonialism in the Americas by Olive Patricia Dickason, University of Alberta Press, 1997.

I made several attempts to contact Winona Linn for this book, but had no success. Her video is available on YouTube: "Winona Linn performing *Marie Angèlique et Moi* at the San Miguel Writers' Conference in San Miguel, Mexico in February, 2017" https://www.youtube.com/watch?v=WV5OU_ivUn8

There's an abundance of material on the web about Cynthia Ann Parker and her connection to *The Searchers*. My main source was Wikipedia.

The Unredeemed Captive, A Family Story from Early America by John Demos, New York: Alfred A. Knopf, 1994.

CHAPTER 10

The Pemoussa quote is from Meskwaki oral tradition and is featured prominently on one wall of the Meskwaki Cultural Center and Museum.

Dakshana Bascaramurty, "Candidates find themselves at centre of debate on Métis identity" in *The Globe and Mail*, October 19, 2019.

Chelsea Vowel and Daryll Leroux, "White Settler Antipathy and the Daniels Decision" in *Topia: Canadian Journal of Cultural Studies*, No. 36, Fall 2016, 30-42.

"Métis Québec Nation, Another View on the Path of a Recognition" by Claude Aubin: http://claudeaubinmetis.com/index.php

Meskwaki Anthology, A Collection of Observations Relating to the Meskwaki Tribe, by Johnathan L, Buffalo, 2004: https://meskwaki.org/about-us/history/

The Indians of Iowa, by Lance Foster, University of Iowa Press, 2009.

Other interesting sources on Meskwaki history and culture:

Wolf That I Am: In Search of the Red Earth People by Fred McTaggart, Houghton Mifflin Harcourt, 1976.

Michael D. Green, "We Dance in Opposite Directions: Mesquakie (Fox) Separatism from Sac and Fox Tribe" in *Ethnohistory*, Vol. 30, No. 3, 1983, 129-140.

"The Last Tribe of Iowa: Leadership of the Meskwaki People in a Struggle for Survival," video by Alex Bare at: https://www.youtube.com/watch?v=gaO-WouB1t0

"Meskwaki Settlement" by the Meskwaki Education NetWork Initiative at: https://www.nrcs.usda.gov/Internet/FSE_DOCUMENTS/nrcs142p2_005480.pdf

CHAPTER 11

I drew information on the Royal Proclamation and the Doctrine of Discovery from online sources, chiefly Wikipedia and *The Canadian Encyclopedia*.

Stolen Continents: Conquest and Resistance in the Americas by Ronald Wright. New York: Penguin Random House, 2015.

Black Hawk: The Battle for the Heart of America by Kerry A. Trask, New York: Henry Holt, 2006.

History of Buchanan County, Iowa. C.S. Percival, Elizabeth Percival, eds. Cleveland: Williams Brothers, 1881.

History of Buchanan County, Iowa and Its People by Harry Church Chappell and Katharyn Joella Allen, Chicago, S. J. Clarke publishing, 1914.

Frederick Douglass: Prophet Of Freedom by David W. Blight, Simon and Schuster, 2018.

The Choctaw Memorial Sculpture "Kindred Spirits" is visible from Bailick Road, south of Midleton City Centre. Read about it at: https://www.irishtimes.com/news/ireland/irish-news/cork-sculpture-recalls-generosity-of-choctaw-nation-during-famine-1.3118580

CHAPTER 12

The Internet has an abundance of resources and personal accounts of visits to the Paris Catacombs. Opinion is quite divided on this tourist attraction. Many find it fascinating, others find it creepy.

In the Footsteps of Abraham Ulrikab, by France Rivet. Polar Horizons, 2014: https://polarhorizons.com/en/abraham-ulrikab
An absorbing account of Rivet's efforts to bring the tragedy of the Labrador Inuit to public attention, which reminded me of my own quest to bring Marie-Angelique's story to light.

CHAPTER 13

The Liffey Swim celebrated its centenary in 2019: http://www.leinsteropensea.ie/liffey-swim/

APPENDIX

THE WOLF SISTERS
by Kathleen McDonnell

Not so many years ago, in a remote village on the edge of a great forest, there lived a teacher. The people of the village were simple, and knew little of the larger world. But the teacher was a learned man who told them of remarkable things and faraway places, where people travelled in horseless carriages on wheels and voices were carried over great distances by thin wires. Though they had much respect for the teacher's knowledge, the people of the village had little interest in his newfangled ideas. They went on living the way of life their parents had lived, and their parents before them.

Wild animals were often seen near the outskirts of the village, and for some time there had been much talk about a pair of unusual creatures that some villagers had seen running with a pack of wolves. A few tried to get up close, to get a better look at the creatures. But they were always driven back by a she-wolf, who guarded the two ferociously. Spirit-wolves, some of the villagers called the strange creatures. The teacher heard the talk, but dismissed it as the usual exaggeration to which the villagers were prone.

Late one night there was a loud pounding on the teacher's door. When he opened it he found a group of villagers holding a large net with two squirming, snarling figures inside. The villagers excitedly told him they had managed to kill the she-wolf and trap the spirit-wolves. They wanted to get advice from the teacher, the wisest man in the village. Were the creatures demons of some kind? Would they bring bad luck to the village? Should they be slaughtered or set free?

The teacher motioned them into the house as the creatures clawed fiercely at the netting.

"Open the net so I can get a better look at them," he said.

It took two or three villagers to restrain each of the creatures as they emerged from the net. The teacher was shocked by what he saw. Except for the long matted manes on their heads, their bodies were smooth and hairless. When he pulled the hair away from their faces he saw bright, piercing eyes. Even in their hideous state, the teacher could see they were not demons, nor even wolves at all.

He let out a cry of astonishment.

"These are children," he told the villagers. "Human children!"

The villagers looked in amazement. It was true. They were human girls. One appeared to be about six or seven years old, the smaller one perhaps four or five. At first the girls raced around the room on all fours. A couple of the villagers tried to put clothes on their naked bodies, but the girls tore at the garments with their teeth and ripped them to shreds. After much struggle, they finally dropped to the floor in exhaustion. They curled up together in a tight ball, growling and twitching as they fell into a deep sleep.

The teacher sent the villagers away, and pondered how the children might have come to be with the wolf pack. He suspected they had been abandoned at birth. People in the village were loath to speak of such things openly. But it sometimes happened that girls from poor families, who would never be able to afford dowries, were put out in the wild shortly after birth. These girls might have been found and suckled by the she-wolf, whose mothering impulses overcame her predatory instincts.

Were they sisters? It was impossible to tell. He did not think it likely that two children, born of the same mother, would have been abandoned at the same time. Perhaps, he speculated, the she-wolf had found one baby, then come across another one like it and adopted her as well. Even if they were not born sisters, it became clear over the days that followed that the two shared a bond closer than twins.

But for all their closeness, the teacher also began to notice some distinct differences between them. The older girl was more assertive, especially in protecting the younger one, who seemed less combative, a bit more adaptable. He resolved to tame the girls and teach them the ways of humans. As a final reminder of the forest which had once been their home, the teacher decided to name the younger girl Fern and the older one Briar.

The true magnitude of the task he had set himself soon became apparent, for the girls seemed to have no trace of humanness in the way they acted and thought. They never smiled or showed any interest in human company. Even their senses were wolf-like. Their eyes glowed in the dark like those of cats, and their hearing was preternaturally sharp. Through much of the day and early evening they slept curled up together in a tight ball, and they would only come awake after the moon rose, when they would howl to be let free.

From the start they resisted all the teacher's attempts at civilizing them. When he tried to make them walk upright, they dropped to all fours and howled. They refused all food but raw meat. When he tried to get them to sit at the table and eat from bowls, the girls knocked them on the floor and got down on all fours to gnaw on the spilled meat. One night, at his wit's end, the teacher put them outside and attached a rope to the foot of each girl. When they realized they could not run away, they began to pace restlessly back and forth, making low growling noises. The teacher turned away and closed the door.

After a time he noticed they had fallen completely silent. Fearful they had somehow gotten free and run off, he peeked out the door. The two girls were sitting perfectly still, listening intently to the distant howl of the wolf pack in the damp night air. The sound seemed to calm them.

Still, there was constant tension between the teacher and his two charges, and they continued to fight him every step of the way. Until finally, after one particularly trying day, it dawned on him that he had been going about things in the wrong way. He couldn't change the girls' habits by force. After all, the only society they had ever known was the wolf pack.

"I, whom the villagers regard as one of the wisest of men, have been a fool."

After all, what did it mean to be human? Was it about sitting at a table? Eating from bowls? No. It was language that truly separated human from beast. The way to reach the wolf sisters, the teacher decided, was through words. If he could teach them to speak, they would be freed from the prison of their animal natures, finally able to fully experience their humanness.

He stopped struggling with the girls. He let them walk on all fours as much as they wanted. He allowed them to eat raw meat and brought them wild plants from the forest. But he spoke to them frequently, always in a clear, calm voice. He addressed each girl by name, and he began to teach them the names for things.

He noticed that, from time to time, Fern seemed to exhibit a genuine curiosity about what he was saying. But more often she followed her older sister's lead, and ignored him completely. His efforts once again seemed to be leading nowhere, and his frustration returned.

One night as the girls lay down to sleep he was moved to sing them a lullaby.

"Hush-a-bye, don't you cry
Go to sleep my little baby.
When you wake you shall have
All the pretty little horses."

As usual, they seemed to have no response, and as they drifted off he began to tiptoe away. Then something stopped him in his tracks.

"Go see bay bee."

Had he heard correctly? He went back to look at the girls. Briar was twitching in her sleep, but Fern looked up at him, wide awake.

He softly sang the lines of the lullaby again. This time Fern sang back to him, the words garbled but recognizable.

"*Go seep il bay bee…*"

The teacher was thunderstruck. "Again!" he commanded. To his great joy, Fern repeated more words from the song.

"*Go seep it-tle bay-bee…*"

He looked over at Briar. She was awake, looking anxious and confused. Fern quickly rolled over, pretending to be asleep. The teacher quietly left the room. Nothing more happened for the next few days. He decided that the sounds Fern made that night had most likely been random vocalizing, without significance. But he continued to sing the lullaby to the girls as they drifted off to sleep at night. One day while Briar was chewing on some meat out in the yard, Fern crept back into the house. She looked up at the teacher and began to sing softly.

"*Hush-a-bye, don't cry*
Go sleep lit-tle baby
When you ay you il have
All pret-ty lit-tle horses."

This time there was no mistaking it. Fern indeed knew the words. The wolf child could speak! And it was equally clear that Fern shared his exhilaration. She was beaming, proud of her newfound ability. But he could also see how much care she took to hide their encounter from Briar, and a chill ran up his spine.

Now Fern's learning began in earnest, and she made remarkable progress. Day by day she mastered more words, at first only through singing but gradually in speech as well. Briar tried to ignore what was going on. They slept intertwined, played together as always. But occasionally the older girl would glance toward the teacher with a look of anger and betrayal.

It seemed to him that Briar understood more than she was letting on. He wondered whether she was as capable of human speech and behaviour as her sister, whether it was simply willful refusal on

Briar's part that kept her from submitting to his teaching. He fervently hoped that she might come around eventually.

One day when the teacher's back was turned, Briar pounced on him without warning, digging her teeth into his leg. Fern leapt over and tried to hold Briar back. Then she did something she had never done before.

"No, Briar!"

Fern had never spoken directly to her before, nor addressed her by name. Briar looked at Fern in shock. Her sister's words were like a brutal slap in the face. Then she turned to the teacher, a look of pure hatred on her face, and skulked out of the room.

That night the wolf sisters slept apart for the first time.

The next morning Fern was careful not to speak in Briar's presence. But the damage was done. A profound gloom settled over the household. The teacher chastised himself for his folly. His great project to humanize the wolf sisters was shattered. What was worse, his actions had brought about a terrible breach between them.

The thing had to come to an end. The girls could not go on living this way, nor he with them. That night he let them both out in the yard without any ropes on their feet, something he had never done before. Then he watched quietly from behind the door.

As the full moon rose, Briar roused Fern. Come! she gestured and tried to drag her sister out of the yard. But Fern resisted and tried to hold her back. In fury Briar threw her off and started toward the forest. But Fern raced after her and blocked her way. For several moments, the two sisters stood looking at one another, as if frozen in time. Then Fern tentatively held out her arms, and Briar allowed herself to be encircled in them. Out of the silence the teacher heard the words of the lullaby he had sung to them that night.

"Hush-a-bye, don't you cry
Go to sleep my little baby
When you wake you shall have
All the pretty little horses."

Fern was singing to her sister.

Overcome with emotion, the teacher turned away and closed the door behind him. When he awoke the next morning, Fern was alone in the yard. She said nothing to him of what had happened.

Briar was never seen in the village again.

Their lives went on much as before. Fern continued to progress, and the teacher raised her as his own daughter. As she grew up, word of Fern's achievements spread to the farthest corners of the earth. She sang with a voice of great otherwordly beauty, and it was said that she even learned to read and write.

Most of the time, Fern seemed happily immersed in her new life. But from time to time, a restlessness would come over her, an unaccountable melancholy. Then she would stand in the doorway when the moon came up, listening to the distant howling of the wolves in the night air.

The sound seemed to calm her.

ACKNOWLEDGEMENTS

I owe an enormous debt to Johnathan Buffalo and Suzanne Wanatee Buffalo for embracing Marie-Angelique into the Meskwaki fold, and for welcoming me into their world.

I want to thank Julia Douthwaite Viglione, for her ground-breaking scholarship and for sharing her own Wild Girl journey with me.

I am deeply grateful to my newfound friends in France, for their gracious hosting and sharing of their knowledge of all things Marie-Angelique: Eric and Marie-Ange Phelizon; Isabelle Guyot and Pierre Gandil at the Bibliotheque Pompidou; Gaëlle Hersent, one of the creators of the BD *Sauvage,* and Francis Passinhas, the Mayor of Songy.

Thanks to dear friends and family members who read the manuscript at various stages of development: Martha Farquhar-McDonnell, Ellen Murray, Annie Szamosi, Alec Farquhar, Linda Rosenbaum. My neighbor and friend Lynn Cunningham did a thorough, thoughtful edit that brought some crucial weaknesses in the draft manuscript to my attention.

Thanks to Bella Cole for valuable help with translation; to Kathy Kacer for steering me to Alex Levin's story; to Roger Bourke for sharing his insights as well as Aroles' manuscript.

Michel Lefebvre was there at the very beginning. His support was crucial, though I expect he's as surprised at where *The Wolf Sisters* has ended up as I am.

Thanks and respect to Franck Rolin, aka Serge Aroles, for his years of painstaking research, upon which this book is built, in hopes of furthering our common aim: to restore this remarkable woman's story to history.

The team at Friesen Press has been wonderful to work with, a fine combination of professionalism and personal support.

I could not have completed this book without the loving support of my daughters Martha and Ivy, my son-in-law Tyler, and my grandson Ciaran (lover of books that he is, I can't wait for him to read this one someday!). But the person whose caring, love and extraordinary skill set has gotten me over the finish line is my spouse Alec Farquhar, who's been my partner-in-crime at every stage of this quest, and whose French is – fortunately – far better than mine will ever be.

Find out more about Kathleen's other books at her website:
www.kathleenmcdonnell.com

CPSIA information can be obtained
at www.ICGtesting.com
Printed in the USA
BVHW032028061120
592524BV00010B/435